Contents

Introduction

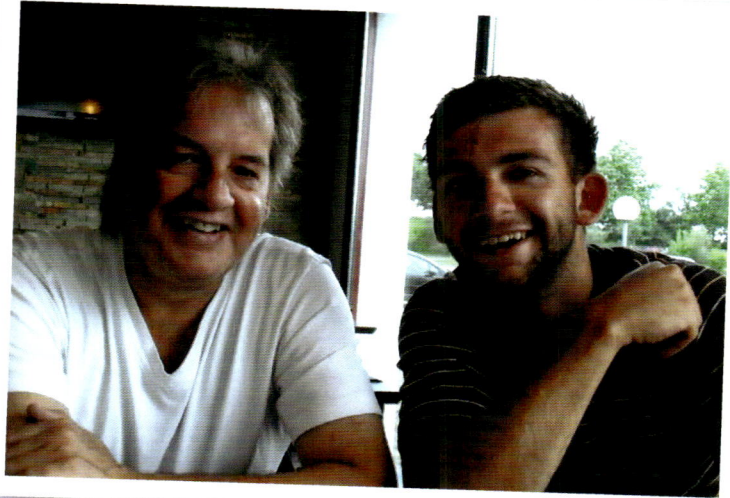

It was July 1998. I was five years old and recovering from a life-changing illness: Meningitis. I was hoisted in the front seat of the car, wheelchair in the boot, and headed down to Bristol to 'take part in the last stage of the' Severn Way 'relay run'. Not only did my Dad organise the hashing event, he wanted ME to take part in it! All in aid of charity: Meningitis Research.

It was then, my earliest memory of running/hashing, that I knew my Dad was completely bonkers for it. In the years that followed, my brother and I tagged along to events to discover my Dad wasn't alone. We had entered a huge community of 'runners' often front running (with our youthful spirit) and engaging with this incredible circle of people.

Dad has often shared stories, predominately anecdotes to family and friends, many of whom can relay their own stories about my Dad and the trips that they'd been on. On occasion a new story would appear that hadn't seen the light of day before. Often followed by a chuckle.

If you're into running, drinking or simply thought about either of the above, it's worth a read!

Craig

Cheltenham & Cotswolds organised a multi-legged relay run along the 224 miles of the Severn Path. The relay was broken into uneven distances as many people wanted to 'run' and take part in raising money. Starting in the wilds and uplands of mid Wales, snaking all the way back to Severn beach, where it originally ended.

However, by extending the route on through Shirehampton and along the Portway, it meant a finish in Hotwells at the Pump House pub. Craig was pushed along the final leg in his wheelchair, enjoying the 'free ride' amidst cheering. We all had a tear in our eye.

'RACE' by Graham Robinson

A jumbled mass of humanity in a thousand shades of hue,
has anybody noticed the length of the queue for the loo?

Various stretching and contortions in readiness for the start,
remember – it's not the winning it's the taking part.

Should I jog some more to see if I can feel that niggle?
I feel pretty self conscious as a group of girls start to giggle.

Its too late now I've just seen the starter, his whistle in hand.
If I get out the blocks it'll all go to plan

The time is approaching a quick gulp of water,
a hot afternoon so I freshen my face.

I just hope I don't finish last in the fathers' race.

It was only recently that I realised just how long I'd been running in some form or other. It will be forty-three years this year 2024. It just crept up on me, I guess. For many years now I have shared the odd anecdote with family and friends, many of whom can remember the incidents and recite them much better than I can. However, every now and then I can recall a 'new episode' which hasn't seen the light of day before. It was on one such occasion that my beloved spouse (after she finished chuckling) suggested that "You should put these in a book".

What rot I thought. Who'd be interested? I quickly dismissed the idea, but more prompting followed. "I've just read a running book best seller" Mrs Robinson continued, "it's not a patch on your tales". "Really?" "You really should give it a go". I still didn't think much about it and so we started on another bottle and tucked further into our candlelit dinner.

Lockdown Literacy

Then in the March of 2020, the world went into meltdown. Kicking off in Wuhan, China, the Coronavirus swept the world, destroying huge populace as it went, running it seemed unchecked. It wasn't however a Sci-Fi of someone's evil imagination, kryptonite didn't cut it. This was a germ that had affected everyone, not just superheroes. For us here in the UK, after PM Boris Johnson closed the pubs, it was the end of civilisation as we knew it. The slogan which heralded the campaign and lockdown was STAY AT HOME, SAVE LIVES, PROTECT THE NHS.

So, would this be the ideal time to while away the boredom and seize the moment? With the memory loss that advancing years brings with them, perhaps now was the moment. You, dear reader can decide.

Whilst not a complete diary, I have attempted to put the events, either a hash event or a race, in chronological order, along with any background or historical fact that might also be of interest. I start by charting early forays, when I wouldn't class myself as a runner, to when I discovered the world of the Hash House Harrier, and somewhere in the middle, help form a bona-fide Athletic Club…

HASH HOUSE HARRIERS –
What does it all mean?

G Spot – Who was Gispert?

Alberto Esteban Ignatio was born of Spanish decent on the 31st July 1903 to parents Arthuro and Remedoes Gispert de Pulguriguer after moving to London in late 1892. 'G' as he was fondly known, and the youngest of seven.

Although brought up in a house which spoke little English, Alberto aquitted himself with English pleasantries and pastimes, which many years later was described by Cecil Lee (one of the four associated with setting up the KL Hash House Harriers) as the perfect English Gentleman.

For it was at his Roman Catholic school on Blackheath, St Josephs Academy, and now closed (2007), where he learnt the basics of the 'paper chase'. This is widely believed to be where the seed was sown and the notion of hashing formulated to manifest many years later.

Indeed that year was 1938 when aged 35 he founded the Hash along with colleagues and friends. In the intervening years G had become an accountant with HD Baker & Co and applied for an overseas posting, working for Evatt & Co (Price Waterhouse) in the Malay capital of Kuala Lumpur. 1937 was a busy year for our hero as he married Eve and had a new born son Simon. Whilst stationed in Malacca he then discovered an already established running club, the Springgit Harriers one of a few paper chase clubs in the region. Again, this previous pastime please was fixed firmly in G's mind.

However, the hash wasn't the first thing on G's mind on his return to KL. No, he first joined the FMSVR (Federated Malay States Volunteer Reserve) who met and trained on a Monday at the Royal Selangor Club. Many civil servants and ex pats were housed in the barracks of this British colonial bastion. After many weeks of cajoling and persuasion G finally got a dozen or so chaps up together for a run. The routine of a regular paper chase after Reserve practice along with a beer or two started to become a 'thing'.

Under strict Malay laws (at the time) any club or social activities had to be licensed. The chaps commented on the meals from the RSC as the hash house as the cuisine was unimaginative, monotonous and barely palatable to western tastes. So as a wheeze upon registering the group G put forward the name of Kuala Lumpur Hash House Harriers. The rest they say is history.

Whilst on duty for the Reserve, during the battle for Singapore, G was killed at Dairy Farm Road early on the morning of 11 February 1942, age 39. His body was never identified. His name is inscribed at the Kranji War Memorial in Singapore on the Memorial Wall. The intervention of the Imperial Japanese Army brought hashing to a stop on 12 December 1941. But in August 1946 the Hash was back with the help of Torch Bennett, Philip Wickens, Cecil Lee and Horse Thompson.

Since then of course, the Hash has become a phenomenon and has spread around the globe. Memorial trails are often laid for the great man's honour. With his home address and family memorial in Brockley Cemetery, South London becoming a shrine to visit. If you do visit the grave – take a beer with you. On On.

Introduction

As a callow youth I thought my Tom Brown schooldays of cross country running were behind me. Those pursuits on wintery afternoons around sodden school playing fields which left your fingers numb, avoiding the mud as best you could to save the archaic cold showers in the boys dilapidated changing rooms… but as it turns out, I hadn't!

The finger of fate prodded me one arctic Sunday morning as a frozen pitch meant my football match was called off. So I was given a lift with some chums to a 'pub and cross country run'. Can you guess which one I was more interested in?

This turned out to be the Cheltenham & Cotswold Hash House Harriers, which was formed in January 1981, and I found myself bumbling along to a run very shortly afterwards, in the March I believe. Here, over time, was where my interest in running was piqued, as the club in the early days attracted a lot of athletes from local running clubs, all looking for another decent run or training effort, followed by a beer.

Hashing was put on hold during WW2, but soon resumed and gained popularity in the Far East before finally spreading globally, reaching the UK in the 1970s.

Both Surrey H3 and Bicester H3 (formed in 1974) still exist, and continue to run regularly. Here in the UK, public houses are used as a start and finish point, with the Hare laying a course in flour, chalk, or occasionally sawdust. The route is always a mystery, and the pack have to navigate their way around to finish back at the pub, with the distance anywhere between 4 and 8 miles.

So that first summer back 'on the run' (1981) was a novel weekly voyage of discovery into countryside I'd never seen and an introduction to pubs I'd never heard of! Any how, all this running meant along the way I got swept up in the recent furore of mass participation running events which sprung up everywhere. So I entered my first and so nearly my last race.

Inaugural UK Nash Hash – Pose for posterity (spot the Author)

Running Log

Event:	**Cheltenham Crack Cancer**
Distance:	**Half Marathon**
Date:	**September 1981**

Following the London Marathon effect (the first being held in April this year), running events started springing up everywhere. The novelty and mass participation event on the doorstep was difficult to resist. Everybody seemed to know about or was running in it, and for an inspiring cause, a CT Scanner for Cheltenham General Hospital. Youthful exuberance meant not much thought or training went into the event. The go-to training shoe at the time was the HI Tech Silver Shadow, although I chose to complete the distance in a pair of Green Flash squash shoes - a bad move. I also discovered 13 miles was a very long way and with the nature of the course a very long uphill slope back toward the finish area at Cheltenham Racecourse. It was a hands and knees finish.

TIME: 2.04

Worcester AC cleaned up that day, and did a number over local runners from Cheltenham & County Harriers.

1) Haywood: 62.04
2) Wood: 66.32
3) Ridout: 66.52

Local pride was restored with Steve Brown finishing 5th: 68.18, and Dave Catlow 9th: 69.25.

The Cheltenham Half Marathon clearly had an effect as it took me two years to recover and attempt anything else.

But wait…

Running Log

Event:	**London Marathon**
Distance:	**26.2 miles**
Date:	**April 1983**

This was my first attempt at the iconic distance of the 26.2 mile marathon course. Although this was the third time the London Marathon was organised, it was a whole lot different back then. Now, some 43 years since its conception, the annual event is part of the fabric of life here in the UK. Who doesn't know a work colleague or an uncle Bob who's not staggered round the course for a charitable cause?

Background

The inspiration for a Marathon race around our capital streets came after founder Chris Brasher had run the New York Marathon in 1979. The New York race had actually started in 1970, but with just 127 competitors running endless laps around central park. It didn't take off as a mass participation event until 1975. In celebration of the USA bicentennial, the Mayor wanted the race to take in all five boroughs, from the start on Staten Island, through Brooklyn, Queens, Manhattan and finally to the finish in Central Park. When Brasher took part in '79 the field numbered just under 10,500. On Brasher's return to the UK that November he spent most of the following year using his persuasive talents, the old boy's network, and some editorial licence, his position as sports editor for the Observer. It did however, take considerable discussions, but he managed to get the GLC, the London boroughs and the police on board with his proposals. He then, along with his lifelong friend John Disley, set about the blueprint for a London equivalent of the already fabled NYC Marathon.

These two masters had a blueprint planned for a field of 4,000. In fact 7000 runners lined up in Greenwich Park on the 29th March 1981. Around

6,255 made it to the finish on Constitutional Hill (just on the corner of Buckingham Palace). It was a wet one with puddles underfoot and overcast skies. If you've ever seen any of the You Tube footage, it looks a gloomy old day.

The inaugural race was an interesting affair, with a fairy-tale finish as Dick Beardsley (USA) and Inge Simonsen (Norway), ran across the finish together holding hands in a time of 2.11.48. Joyce Smith, a 43 year-old housewife won the ladies race with 2.59.58, a then British record.

As with any London Marathon, such is the magnitude that the process starts in the Autumn before the race itself, generally October with yes, you've guessed it, the ballot (although these days it's a lottery). The training is actually the easiest part, especially as the event these days is so oversubscribed with some 480,000 entries for some 40,000 places. When you factor in guaranteed Charity runners and celebrities participating, that number dwindles even further. But as with everything in life (it seems), it wasn't always like that.

> Which takes you to the start of my first London Marathon.

My race was in its final year of sponsorship by Gillette and it marked a couple of bumps in the road. First, the floodgates were thrown open by the IAAF, when it breathtakingly allowed athletes to be paid start money. This meant spiralling costs for all major marathons as top athletes would be attracted by the most lucrative deals. Second, it was also the first race which saw wheelchair competitors take part. Brasher was dead set against this introduction, wanting to keep it a pure athletics race. However, the GLC had other ideas with Ken Livingstone threatening to remove funding. For the 1983 London Marathon, applications were received from some 60,000 would-be entrants. 18,000 were accepted with 16,500 making the start line. The mention of applications is really where

A mass participation start seen here pulling away from Greenwich, London

the nub of my story lies. As I hinted, things were very different back in the 1980s. For a start you had to send off in the post to a London PO Box number to receive your entry form.

Online applications were nearly thirty years away with technology not coming on stream to PCs until 2009.

I'd sent off for my entry form and it duly arrived. It also came with an entry open date. Now the trick, back in those days, was to get it into the postal system early, as successful applications were determined on the receipt of the earliest date and time-stamped form. Yes, simply first come, first served. Being in the capital helped naturally, but we had come up with another wheeze. Back in 1983 Cheltenham's town centre in the Promenade (opposite Cavendish House), was the General Post Office, Cheltenham's principle sorting depot. So we figured that the greatest opportunity of a guaranteed entry was to get our forms in the moment the post office opened for business.

Myself and others from the local Hash - Cheltenham & Cotswold, deduced that we would have to camp out overnight to ensure we would be first. A rota was devised and the advance party took up their place on the pavement, in deckchairs, from 6pm the day before! It was a worthwhile decision as we weren't the only group who had come up with that cunning plan. Operating in shifts, we went through the night, proving great amusement to the revellers leaving the clubs at two in the morning. At 4am somebody produced a football, so we picked a couple of teams and had a kick about in the road. Dawn broke and after a night of shivering in our sleeping bags and deck chairs the moment had arrived. The Post Official General slid back the brass plate and in we piled with our entries – we were in!

The prospect of a race weekend in London was very exciting. We were staying in the Strand Palace Hotel - one of the many weekend packages which hotel chains latched onto around the event. Our hash group managed to persuade the hotel to let us make use of a room until 4pm, ideal to get back and have a post-race soak in the bath and leave any baggage. A warm sunny Saturday meant a sight-seeing tour and several pubs to boot (I was a complete novice and the Marathon didn't get my full respect on that first occasion). This wasn't perhaps the wisest thing to do. Sunday would prove to be a Long Hard Road. No coincidence that Ron Hill would use that as a title to his autobiography.

Race day turned out to be a wet and cold morning and that, together with nursing a muzzy hangover, Greenwich Park wasn't the jamboree I had envisaged. Heavy rain was bouncing off the start line, and the go-to outfit was the ubiquitous black bin liner. I was so cold and wet I ran the first 17 miles still cocooned in it.

Black Bin Liners were all the rage

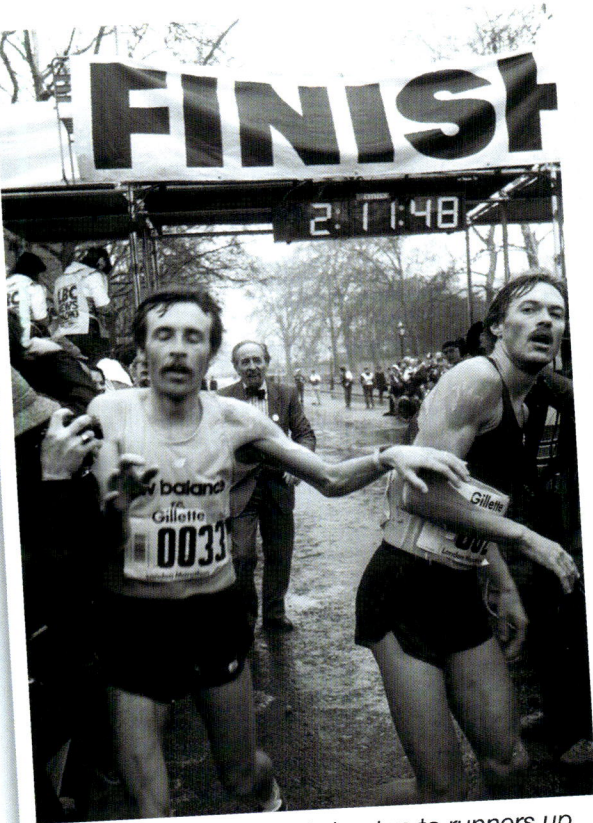

Man in bow tie narrowly beaten to runners up place behind Beardsley and Simonsen

One of the things I do remember was the wastelands of the bleak, crumbling East India docklands and abandoned warehousing of the Isle of dogs. This trudge was roughly between 14 and 19 miles and had NO spectator support. Even TV coverage was sparse for those at home watching on TV! Back in 1983 there was no tube line (remember the first signs of a Docklands Light Railway didn't come along until 1987). You were at a low ebb and many runners hit the wall in this section. In the Dogs no one could see you cry.

After the original London Marathon, certain tweaks were incorporated with the course, mainly as numbers increased, and to avoid certain pinch-points. My run that day finished with what I consider to be the best finish of a London Marathon course. Rather than running the entire length of the Embankment, halfway along the Embankment the route took a right, down Northumberland Avenue and out into Trafalgar Square.

This helped enormously as psychologically that long, long, drag along the Embankment (which I endured in later years), seemed to go on forever. The route now jinked left under Admiralty Arch, then down the Mall towards Buckingham Palace. The finish was on Westminster Bridge, so a left at the fountains and a final push along Bird Cage Walk. The target was now Big Ben. The tube station entrance on the corner was the 26-mile marker, now just pile it on for the final 385 yards. The camber of Westminster Bridge made it an uphill finish so it was a tough final ask.

The space blanket (and the medal) were welcome accessories, but it was the chocolate bar I was most grateful for. A Nestlé Crunch bar (Yum)

TIME: 4.01

Up Front That Day

For the TV audience it was an intriguing race. Mike Gratton proved tough enough to withstand the challenge of an inspired Gerry Helme to win in 2:09:43. The two English guys had hit the front after making their way through the pack in the early stages of the race and were shoulder to shoulder as they reached the Tower of London. When Gratton sensed that Helme was suffering even more than he was, he made his move, across the cobbles, opening a lead that was never reduced. Helme, with a personal best of 2:14:51 before the race, finished second in 2:10:12. Third that day was Henrik Jorgensen from Denmark, who subsequently won the 1988 London. Sadly, Henrik died on Bornholm (Island in Denmark) in January 2019 aged 57, from a heart attack during a training run.

Here Come The Girls

A foot-perfect Waitz debut - Grete Waitz, the world's finest woman marathon runner (maybe), made her London debut and won easily in 2:25:29. It lasted as a world's best for less than 24 hours as American Joan Benoit ran even faster in Boston the following day. Two GB women to make their mark a year later were Sarah Rowell and Priscilla Welch, finishing 9th and 10th respectively.

Winners:
Mike Gratton, England : 2.09.43
Grete Waitz, Norway : 2.25.29

60,000 entered, 16,500 started.

Ron Hill

For many runners of a certain generation, Ron Hill was an inspiration. He was for my early interest in marathon running, or was it the clothing line he produced? Or was it his best seller (for the aspiring runner) his book The Long Hard Road?

Ron was certainly old school, but in the late 1960's and 70's he set dozens of records at every level, except, ironically, the marathon. He did win major honours and won gold medals for the marathon at the 1969 European Championships in Athens and in 1970 won gold at the Commonwealth Games in Edinburgh. However, many would call his victory in the 1970 Boston marathon his BIGGEST achievement.

Ron was invited to run Boston in 1970 after setting a course record in the Athens marathon. There was just one problem: Ron couldn't afford the air fare to America. In those days no prize money was available and prizes would be in the form of gifts, such as a picnic hamper or a set of bed sheets from the race sponsor. Anyway, somehow Ron cobbled the money together via a whip-round from his home town (the old-school equivalent of crowd-funding).

Boston is famed for not just the tea party. The Boston marathon is the worlds oldest annual marathon (save for Covid!), which started in 1897 following the successful Olympic marathon the previous year. It is unfortunately now also remembered for the awful terrorist attack at the finish line in 2013.

Having got there, Ron had nowhere to stay, there was no sponsor to accommodate him in a swanky hotel suite. Lucky Ron had such sway that the Organiser, Jock Semple, met him off the plane and he took him home to stay with his family. Come race day it it rained. Not just just rained, but poured. Even considering he was running most of the way into a headwind, he won. His time was 2.10.30, a course record then. His quotes are interesting at the

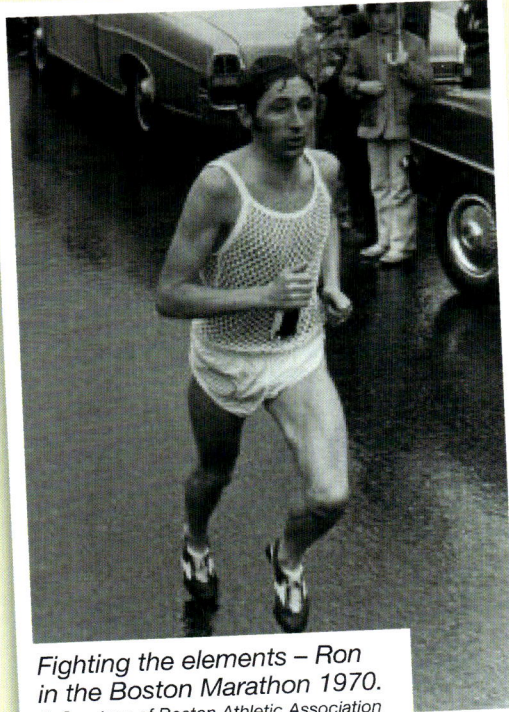

Fighting the elements – Ron in the Boston Marathon 1970.
© Courtesy of Boston Athletic Association

time: 'I had no idea what time I was running. I didn't have a watch and the mile markers were weird, like the one that said '4 ¾ miles to go'. I couldn't believe it when I found I'd run a 2:10 personal best. For winning, I got a medal and a bowl of beef stew,"

Born in 1938, Ron was a fascinating throw-back to the days when marathoners were forbidden to drink water before the ten mile mark. "The rules were strict," he says. "If a spectator offered a cup of water you didn't dare take it - if an official spotted you, you'd be thrown out of the race."

The Streak

Who in the 1980's didn't have the sartorial elegance of the Ron Hill string vest and Union Jack running shorts – just me then? It's for his incredible running streak of 52 years and 39 days - without a day off. He ran around airport terminals when stuck in transit for hours. He broke a leg and hopped around the block for a mile.

It seemed like it was over for The Streak in the nineties, when a head-on car crash could have meant the end, as it left him with his sternum broken in two places. "Fortunately I'd already run that morning," he says. "They let me out of hospital the next day—and when my wife and mother went out to do grocery shopping I sneaked out and did a mile. I could feel the bones moving around."

Today, long after the end of his competitive career, he's still held in awe in running circles around the world because of 'The Streak.' Ron went for a 10 mile training run on 20th December 1964 – and didn't miss a single day until ill health stopped him in 2017. Incidentally, that streak was 59 years and 39 days. He had bunion surgery, and yet managed a mile in a plaster cast every day for the next week, hobbling on a cane for 27 minutes.

Ron Hill - a marathon icon, and personal inspiration, died in May 2021 aged 82.

Jogging Along in the Background

As the Eighties rolled on I became more interested in running, something I'd had no real interest in, certainly not since my school days. Besides, football was my chosen sport, and one which I'd had some minor (local) success in.

An exploratory meeting was being held in a local youth club, which was to be used to gauge what interest there might be in forming a running club. I popped along and in 1984 I helped set up Tewkesbury Athletic Club (as it was then called), along with luminaries such as Josh Gilder, Martin Berry, Geoff Webb, and Bill Kirkwood (and a couple of others whose names escape me).

These guys took the running lark a bit more seriously than I had previously, and had training nights and handicapped events based at the towns YMCA on a Wednesday night. Plenty of advice was on hand and a real camaraderie was built up in those early years. Especially in the YMCA bar after an 8 mile training session.

My main focus remained as running with and developing the local Hash House Harrier group – Cheltenham & Cotswold. I was Trail Master (person who oversees the calendar of runs and keeps an eye on the standard), a stint which lasted for five years. This was followed by being Grand Master for a further five years, where I organised several Jamboree festival weekends of hashing (and some running), as well as the Blue Ribbon event of a UK Nash Hash, held at Rendcomb College, where we had 640 attendees.

I did start to represent Tewkesbury AC in a number of events, especially team relays and cross country. Mainly in the B team, but I was dead chuffed to do so, and tried to uphold the honour of the Black & Gold. It lead me to some memorable race moments, as I hope you'll discover as you read on.

Tewkesbury Running Club - Born again Athlete

Formally Tewkesbury AC, the club was formed in 1983 with a meeting held in a local Boys Club to gauge the interest. It was at this meeting I and others helped get the club off the ground, and I supported it whenever I could. This often meant turning out for 'events' which were an uncomfortable distance or as a time-honoured Marshall, standing out on the cross-country course in all winds and weather.

I was cordially invited along with some other originals, as a guest to the club's 25th Anniversary Dinner in 2009 at the Gupshill Manor in Tewkesbury. Some of us were delighted to discover our roads' best times were still holding up against today's' lean, mean, modern competitor.

N.E.W. Hash, NEW Beginnings

Life gives you a bump to earth from time to time and in the summer of 2018 one such experience occurred when I found myself ostracised from my regular hash group. This was a chastening experience, for not only myself, but my wife and family and friends.

A few months went by with no running (hashing) when gradually I was persuaded to get back out there again. So in January 2019 after much encouragement and support we founded a new Hash group. The North East West Cotswolds HHH. The previous group becoming more and more sedentary we decided to put the accent firmly on the running front, encouraging people to run and jog at what ever pace they can manage. As a result it has rekindled my interest and joy once more for running.

Running Log

Event: King Street Run
Distance: Cambridge HHH 300th Run
Date: July 1984

A run certainly, but one with a difference. And alas, a time-honoured event which has been lost to the mists of time. In those days what we deemed a lark is now classified as unsocial behaviour and binge drinking. But we had a lot of fun doing it, and for many hashers it was another rite of passage.

For the Cambridge HHH weekend run and celebration of 300 runs, the body of the hash had decamped out of the city to the wilds of East Cambridgeshire, where a sea of tents had surrounded the village hall. On the Friday evening back in town was the curtain raiser: The legendary and infamous King Street Run.

Although my 1984 attempt is documented here, let's first give you the context and background to this archetypal eccentric English folly. This evening dates back to the 1950s, when two groups of students - one a group of medical students, and the other a trio of undergraduates at St John's College - were out drinking in the town. A discussion started up with the Medical students from St Johns as to whether the maximum capacity of the male bladder was 4 pints. It was disputed of course and to settle the argument a 'test challenge' was set up for the following weekend. King Street was chosen as it simply had (at the time) fourteen pubs, and so a half in each was the target, with the side issue of no peeing or puking along the route.

THE KING STREET RUN

Cambridge students being Cambridge students, rules were drawn up, including the imposition of a penalty on anyone guilty of urinating, or vomiting. The penalty? Drinking yet another pint of beer.

The pub crawl these days is very much out of vogue, whereas a boys own, it was a staple of a stag night before the nuptials, or indeed a student rag. The King Street Run however takes it to a whole different level of a drinking bout, and it's thanks to the intellectual machinations of University undergraduates.

Thus the event became a rite of passage for the first termers' passing through the hallowed hall of learning. But, before I regale you of my drunken KSR attempt, I'd like to introduce you to the words of R. Wellesly Burton and take you back to a more gentile time…

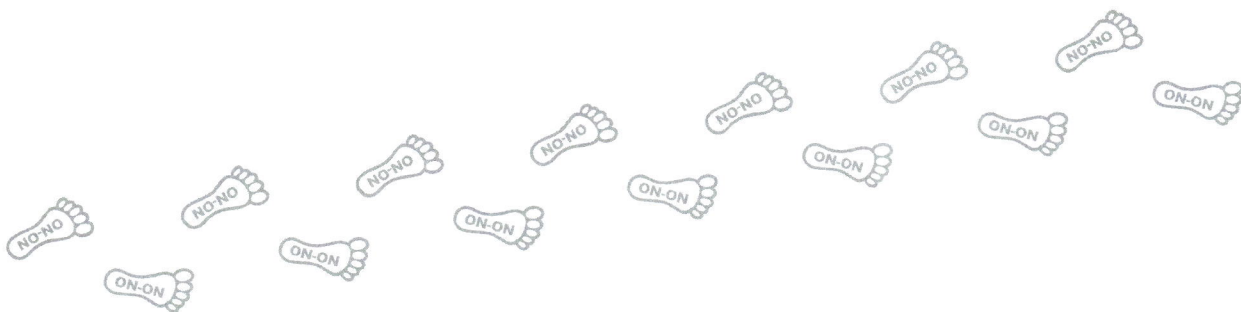

TALES OF OLD KING STREET

Way back in 1963 I was secretary of the original King Street Runners or King Street Pint to Pint to give it its full name. The KSR was to become known as a drinking contest to down 8 pints in a series of pubs along the route. But back in the late 1950s it was viewed as a University social club (very much like the Hash House Harriers) where the Run was an initiation test to show that you were a compatible good chap. The resulting 'badge of honour' - a KSR necktie - could be worn in any of the undergraduate tolerant pubs in Cambridge and be sure of finding kindred spirts.

Pubs were pubs in those days. The Blue Boar, The Red Lion, The Bath, The Eagle and The Fountain were proper drinking houses. Each had several bars with a genteel one for sipping a sherry with your parents, a secluded one for serious courting, and a bare one for serious drinking. All staffed by white-coated barmen who picked up the young gentlemen when they fell over. In my final year as an undergraduate the pride in belonging to this exclusive club was being lost (also the run was going into a decline as the old social atmosphere was being lost as young pretenders came to do the KSR wet behind the ears on arrival and very soon wet all down the front of their shirts when they left – never to be seen again).

But I digress… there were two Runs per term, starting at the Duke of Cambridge. It was my duty (as Secretary) to read out the rules to the assembled throng. Unfortunately, I lost both the rule book and even my tie! (this I swapped with a Russian Seaman I met in the Antarctic for a fur-lined hat and a packet of Sputnik cigarettes).

The rules in general outlined the route and the organisation of the event, however there was one very important injunction that "Parking a tiger in a piano, trumpet, trombone or any other musical instrumental shall lead to instant disqualification". This recalled a regrettable incident in pub number 8 (The Prince of Wales), which was in a basement. One novice was taken short and falling to make it up the stairs, threw up in a Grand piano. The wretched instrument had to be completely stripped down for cleaning and retuning. The runners, understandably banned forever and a day.

Every novice was accompanied by a 'whipper in' who brought the beer in advance and acted as adjudicator. Notable fast times were under 30 minutes, but I took over an hour, as I absent-mindedly stopped for a game of darts in the Champion of the Thames. (ed. No time limit in those days). It did get a bit lively on occasion - I remember a Railway guard getting very upset having had a pint emptied in his upturned peaked BR cap.

However, possibly the worst incident was on the night one poor lad had been persuaded to take part - against his will - had succumbed to the cajoling and already had a couple before 'joining in'. By the end of the evening he needed a supporter each side to prop him up. The last pint was administered by his whipper, by slapping him in the face and tipping in the beer when he let out a scream.

Eventually we had to carry him home, and while resting in a doorway, a police van turned up and wheeled him away (I'm sorry sir, there has been a complaint). However, on return to the taverns, the support team was lucky to avoid being 'progged'. The university Proctor had just arrived and was taking names. Whether this role is still held in the University I'm unsure but, in those days, the UP's wore top hats and tail coats and referred to us as 'sir' (it was much more civilised back then).

Polite notices would go up in college, such as "Gentlemen coming in late are reminded that it is an offence to lift the gates off their hinges".

However, the days of the King St Run were numbered, as both civil and academic rules were put into force which saw the end (in that guise at least) and it was banned by the late 1960s. By then however, students had found other ways to revolt.

R. Wellesley Burton

Resurrection

It was the announcement in the Cambridge Paper two years earlier for the Cambridge HHH 200th run which alerted the local CAMRA group (campaign for real Ale) that the fabled Run should be resurrected as, after several decades, five of the original King St pubs were now selling Real Ale again. The hash duly obliged and with tweaks to the original format set the KSR running again. It had its' demise in the 1960s as interest declined, and much rebuilding took place in the street, and in 1982 just 5 pubs remained. Interestingly enough, with a bit of foot and detective work, an old tailor's shop was found which incredibly still had a large stock of the original KSR ties. He was dumbfounded in the sudden interest: he hadn't sold a tie in years. After Cambridge Hash House Harriers resurrected the run in 1982, the event was staged every two years at centenary celebrations. The precursor to the weekend being the KSR on the Friday evening.

Souvenir Weekend T shirt

It was two years later when I got across to partake in the King St Run for the Cambridge HHH 300th celebrations being held at Stetchworth. This appealed to me. It's a beerly challenge and one of those bucket list options which occasionally crops up in the zany world of hash. Besides, back then as a young buck who could shift a pint or two, I fancied my chances. I'd been christened (in the name of the hash) earning my moniker following the unsuccessful attempt to down 2.5 imperial pint measure on stage in the bi-annual UK Nash Hash Down Down competition in 1983 at Croxton Park. I didn't manage to down it in one, but I almost drowned in the torrent of best bitter I tipped all down me. On my return to Cheltenham Hash the following week I was duly christened 'The Human Sponge'. There was much excitement on Midsummer Common as the who's who of hash had gathered at the Fort St George, the Cambridge H3 official watering hole. I sidled inside and found a throng around a beer-stained table as participants were signed in and

duly elected a Steward (minder). I was also briefly introduced to who I would be lodging with that evening (Colonel John Turville), but would I ever set eyes on him again or even recognise him after 8 pints? It was typical Cambridge H3 (Bear Dosanjh) organisation at its finest. With minders sorted they were given 10 minutes start to get the first pub to ready the beers. I had been paired up with Hong Kong Joe, as the twenty or so Hashletes lined up.

3, 2, 1, GO! I won the race down to the first pub and the St Rad, I was the first entrant into the tiny snug (my only claim to success that evening). I was amongst the early leaders of mainly Wessex H3, including John Philips no less, followed by North Hants (Bill Kerr) along with Guerney and Timbo (Surrey H3). The advantage I gained was lost immediately as the beers hadn't been pulled off.

We caught the startled landlord off guard and had to wait while the beers were readied. The course from the olden days had to be modified, so using a 2-circuit approach to get in the eight pint quota, that's four pubs twice. A start in the St Radegund, then down to the Champion of the Thames, then the Bun Shop, before nipping across to the King Street Run Pub (formally Horse & Groom), then repeating before finishing back at the end of King Street and the St Radegund.

I did struggle with the strange local brews - I was used to old fashioned Whitbread's or even Wadworth's - this was flat dark Anglian ale. I was just about able to gulp down the Green King IPA medicine, but as for the Tolly Cobbold, I hated the taste and what's worst, in two pubs time I had to try and stomach another one. Ohh, for a lager shandy!

Time was slipping by, remember that 1 hour time limit, but John 'Cripple' Phillips (the bookies favourite) was already back at the finishing pub and about to shatter the course record. Down it went in 24 minutes flat (and just the beer). But wait - were congratulations premature? As in the man mountain of Derek Lynn (Wessex) hove into view, if he could just knock back his last pint it would be an incredible 22 minutes. He didn't manage it and by all accounts chundered and sprayed the pavement and road more widely than a council cleansing lorry!

My Chinese minder, Hong Kong Joe, was very good at talking as a distraction device, not so hot on timekeeping, and I managed to stumble up to the St Radegund for pint eight, but right on the hour and in a bit of a state. I had to down the horrible concoction in about 10 seconds flat. I sunk it, but had to keep it down. I now had 2 (pissed) official adjudicators studying my every movement. I couldn't help it, I belched and a miniscule amount of beer spilled out. The over zealous idiots ruled I'd threw up and was disqualified, I had no reproach unless I drank a 'penalty pint' to complete the course.

I declined the offer in no uncertain terms, and I did feel cheated, but made a real hash pal in Hong Kong Joe.

There are currently only four pubs left in King Street:
- The King Street Run (86 King Street, previously named The Horse and Groom and dating back to at least the 1830s)

- The Champion of the Thames (68 King Street, in use as a pub since the late 1860s)

- St Radegund (129 King Street, built in 1880 on part of the site of the Garrick Hotel) named after the sixth-century Saint, Radegund

- The Cambridge Brew House (1 King Street, previously the Jolly Scholar, the Bun Shop, the Kings Arms, the Royal Arms), built in the 1970s.

The current record is 24 min 05 sec, held by John Philips of the Wessex Hash House Harriers.

Running Log

Event: **Stroud Half Marathon**
Distance: **13.5 miles**
Date: **28th October 1984**

28th October 1984 was the third running of the Stroud Half Marathon. The finishing sprint and funnel was then in the main school entrance Marling School.

STROUD HALF-MARATHON 1984

Running Log

Event: **Gloucester Black Bridge Road**
Distance: **Relay**
Date: **2.5 mile**

Starting and finishing on the old cinder track at the Crypt school this a four man team event each leg comprising of a 2.5 mile run. This was a fast and ferocious event taking in the local housing estate and back starting and finishing on the track.

I had taken my recently married spouse for a shopping and lunch outing in the city beforehand, so I pitched up just in time to see the first runner set off. I was awarded the third man slot, just enough time to digest my liquid lunch.

TIME: 16.40

Running Log

Event: **Carrington Hall**
Distance: **(Gloucester Half Marathon)**
Date: **March**

This race was ran out in 'the sticks', around B roads near Frampton-on-Severn. I used this event as a training run, as unusually, the race took place in the afternoon. I did a sharp seven mile run in the morning which added to the brisk thirteen as prep for my up and coming marathon.

TIME: 1.32.34

Running Log

Event: **Wolverhampton Marathon**
Distance: **Marathon**
Date: **6th April**

Whilst not the perfect run, this race produced my PB at this distance. The Wolverhampton was a BIG deal back then, equally on par with the London Marathon. It was a top quality event. The architect was Billy Wilson, an ex-marine who went on to dream up and organise the original Tough Guy, in aid of Tettenhall Horse Sanctuary Foundation. The race actually started in a snow storm. As we made our way to the first feed station a covering of snow had settled on the pavements. As the weather can so easily change, the second half of the race was completed in warm spring sunshine.

At twenty miles I was inside a 2.50 finishing time, but alas crashed into the dreaded wall at 22 miles. I had to jog and walk over the next couple of miles as the route was very sparse of any spectators or landmarks to lift my spirits, let alone my legs. Eventually I did get going again and finished well.

TIME: 3.13.34 - all time PB.

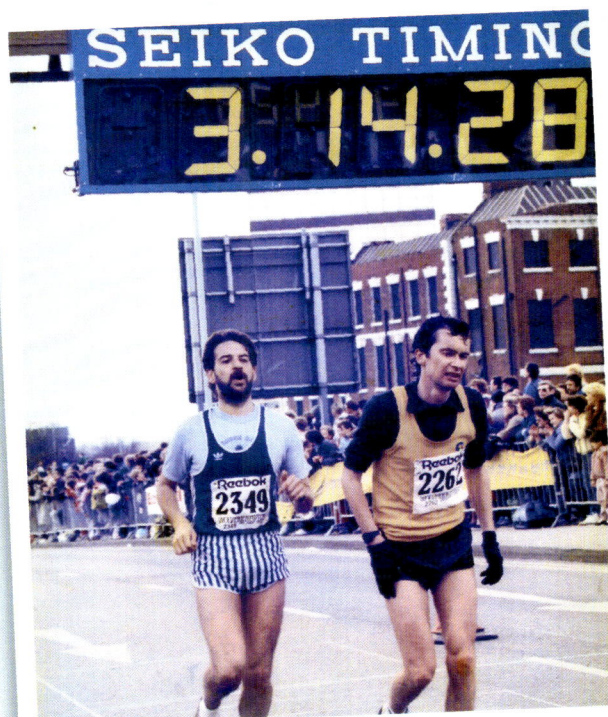

Getting it over the line at Wolverhampton

Snakes and Ladders

I've been laying hash trails and trying to out-smart the average FRB (Front Running Bastard) since the beginning of the 1980s. The art of subterfuge is all part of the Hares' armoury. Sometimes I've used an A-B course, with the pack having no clue of destination B, but with a double bluff of running them back to where they started, worked a treat.

I once sent a pack right through a friends house. I led them right up the garden path - literally. The trail ran through the back gate, up said garden path, in the kitchen door, up the hallway, and out through the front door. We did lay sheets of newspaper on the hall carpet as protection against muddy trainers. Another wheeze was to catch a train.

This didn't work so well on the evening however. Set in Malvern Spa with two train stations you can catch one train at one station (Malvern Link) and alight at the other (Great Malvern). It was a wet Halloween night and upon arriving at Malvern Link we discovered that the train was delayed. So we had to huddle in the waiting room while the train limped into platform 2.

One madcap idea I had was to use a set of ladders, which although worked famously, landed me in hot water with the boys in blue. But, like all good tales, let's start at the very beginning. The trail had been reccied and sussed over a few weeks, and was set in and around the town of Tewkesbury. The route took in some of the summer meadows near the River Severn and was due to loop back round from the north of the town along a disused and overgrown railway line, perfect hash trail. Even better - when I had been out exploring the route, originally the line ran through a tunnel (Mythe Tunnel). I ventured into the cavernous tunnel which after a few hundred feet was pitch dark.

Once my eyes had become accustomed to the light (lack of) I went on a little further to observe at the end of the tunnel it had been bricked up. But only up three quarters of the way and daylight was visible. It was then I had a notion. I quickly nipped out of the tunnel and following the footpath out and around I made my way up over the road, past the nurseries over the A38 to find the other end of the tunnel, and there it was.

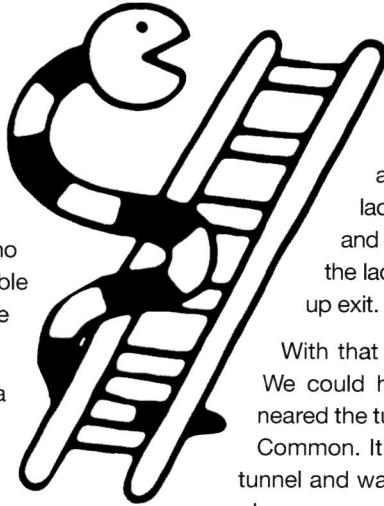

What if we made the pack run into the tunnel and then get them to climb out using some ladders? It sounded a fab idea, they won't expect that. Now all I had to do was get hold of some ladders. The trail was a Monday evening and so earlier in the day my co Hare and I hid the ladders in the undergrowth at the blocked up exit.

With that job done off we went to lay the trail. We could hardly contain ourselves as the pack neared the tunnel after the loop across Shuthonger Common. It worked a treat, no-one expected the tunnel and was stunned when confronted when the only escape was up and over with some ladders, it really was quiet a hoot. So all back in the bar and a satisfaction of a plan coming together and adding something a bit different. No harm done. So that was on the Monday.

Tuesday evening while at home the doorbell goes. I open the door to two strangers in suits (oh no, not JWs is my first thought).

Mr Robinson? Yes.

Is this your van sir? (my company van's parked on the drive.) Yes.

Where you aware it was parked in the vicinity of the Mythe yesterday afternoon? Yes.

Now what's this about? Had I broken some by-law? Parked on private property? My mind was racing for a plausible reason why two plain-clothed policemen are on my doorstep.

Can you explain what you were doing with a set of ladders? Oh - you mean the hash! I couldn't help but just blurted it out, more in relief that on my part it was just innocent jinx.

'Hash' Sir? Can you explain? Perhaps we better have a word inside.

I then spent the next two hours trying to convince the oversensitive CID that I wasn't an international drug runner, operating a county line. It transpires there was a watching brief on the tunnel as contraband and drugs are stowed in the tunnel to be moved on. They had missed 30 hashers scaling a wall with ladders in broad daylight, but some snake had reported us in any case.

Running Log

Event:	**Seven Sisters Marathon**
Distance:	**26.2 miles**
Date:	**28th February**

Originally this event was a strict walking event, organised by the LDWA (Long Distance Walkers Association). However, on some events the LDWA allowed runners to participate. In the Seven Sisters instance it began life in February 1981. What seemed like a huge crowd of 182 walkers set off at 8am, then later 68 runners followed, and within half a mile or so vanished into a thick sea fog while clutching their route descriptions, many went astray in the first few miles!

These LDWA events were all self navigation with rudimentary sketch maps and route descriptions, dyed in the wool runners weren't used to such things, and were still light years away from GPS Strava etc... However, this hiccup didn't deter the take up, and club runners wanting something a little different. The event grew so popular that in 1985 the Sussex group had to impose a limit of 2,000. By the time I entered the event had grown so much that just a map was issued with route markers on the course, plus the odd marshal. It was also increased in length to the correct full marathon distance.

The year I took part you were still given a sketch map (just in case). The race started just outside Saint Bedes school with a very steep, practically vertical start. The course could be described as undulating as if you're not descending of the South Downs, then you're making your way back up and over them. The golf course is negotiated first, 6 miles its Friston Forest. After a couple of hours you spend much of the time running on your own. If you're lucky you may spot a runner up in front to zone in on, but it may take you 20 minutes or so to catch up to them, and then it's generally at a checkpoint. These are very welcome and then by

'No roads' Marathon

THE Seven Sisters marathon is a unique race over the full marathon distance in that no roads are used.

Local runner Graham 'Robbo' Robinson decided to make the long journey to Eastbourne to take part.

Robbo found the course tough but very satisfying. His endurance was rewarded with a highly commendable finishing position of 197th out of about 1,000.

Robbo thoroughly recommends the race to any runner who wants to try something different. It follows the South Downs Way footpath and is named after the Seven Cliffs that it crosses, the most famous of which is Beachy Head.

Gloucestershire Echo

volunteers from the sea cadets all local Rotary club. Alfriston is a picturesque village you trot through, the pub is tempting, but I push on past.

East Dean is another checkpoint, but the one I linger at the most is at the Biring Gap. Here, the ladies had provided lashings of sweet tea and Dundee cake. Yum. At this point I was still on for a sub four-hour finish, which is no mean feat. This was easily the toughest endurance event I'd ever undertaken. Just the iconic Seven Sisters to negotiate now. The steep rise and fall of the cliffs did take it to all, whilst I did stop to look at the Beachy head Lighthouse, I didn't contemplating jumping off. The time had gone and I just wanted to finish in one piece now. The said steep start was part of the finish, although you had to go into the school itself, the main hall where you are officially classed as completed at the registration table and given your time.

TIME: 4.03.08

The 21st event was run in October 2001 and was sadly thought to be the last Seven Sisters organised by Les Smith. Fortunately, the event was saved by new organisers Nicola Williams and Hugh Graham. It was however re-branded and called the Beachy Head Marathon and now offers 4 different lengths; 10k through to Ultra Marathon.

Running Log

Event:	**Bath Half Marathon**
Distance:	**13.1 miles**
Date:	**15th March**

TIME: 1.27.42

Adidas Mars Bath marathon
Adidas and Mars are jointly sponsoring a series of Half Marathon races throughout the UK again this year. The first was held at Bath on 15th March in fine but breezy conditions. Barry Mumford and Bill Kirkwood were particularly successful.

Both recorded personal best times, Barry making a massive improvement of about 2 minutes.

Tewkesbury runners, with positions and times, were Barry Mumford (267 -77.23), Bill Kirkwood (298 -78.06), Gary Avery (492 -81.15), Martin Berry (929 -87,32), G. 'Robbo' Robinson (945 - 87.41) and Geoff Webb (1283 - 92.12). There were about 2300 starters for the race.

Gloucester A.C. Road Relays.
Tewkesbury A.C fielded two teams in the annual 4 x 2 mile relays at Black Bridge.

Although the A team of A Dumper, B. Kirkwood, M. Perry, and M. Peakman were placed higher overall the B team had the last laugh as they came away with prizes as the third placed all veterans team (over 40s).

The successful 'B' team were Alan Chandler, Gary Avery, Gerry Portman and Mike Hawker.

Gloucestershire Echo

Running Log

Event:	**Tewkesbury Half Marathon**
Distance:	**13.1 miles**
Date:	**May**

A rain-lashed event, which back then was organised by the local authority, with its start and finish at the council offices. This didn't affect my run too much as I posted my fastest time at the distance.

TIME: 1.25.53 PB

Splashing up Tewkesbury High Street, proudly wearing the black and gold colours in my 'home' race.

Running Log

Event:	**Offa's Dyke**
Distance:	**15 miles Fell Race (Category C),**
Date:	**June**

After a few years racing on the roads, my interest declined in just shaving off seconds for a PB in the local race scene. So I looked further afield, to discover an as-yet-unheard-of running category - the Multi Terrain event. I'm not sure how I got to hear about this race, possibly a race flyer slipped under my windscreen wiper. Anyhow, the idea appealed. Of course we all know that Offa's Dyke is now a National Trail (NT) which runs from Prestatyn to Sedbury (Chepstow), and is some 177 miles in length. Whilst not the longest NT in the UK, it could be considered the most arduous, incorporating some mountainous ranges and isolated hamlets in forgotten valleys.

The race itself was (is) a fifteen mile section starting in Hay-on-Wye and finishing in Kington. Yes, an A-B race. It was also an afternoon race, so plenty of time to arrive in the Welsh hillsides and get my head around the logistics of stowing my car at the finish, and, along with umpteen others, cram into a Land Rover back to the start. It was a blistering hot day and I chose to wear my 'Ron Hill string vest' for the occasion. The race started in the centre of Hay next to the Clock Tower, dropping down through the town and crossing over the stone bridge and the River Wye.

Early on the running is through meadows, with the trajectory maintaining an upward tilt. After reaching Newchurch it is very much fell running, short, sharp descents were the most difficult, down loose shale and rocks. My trainers weren't up to the job as wizened old runners leaped past with springs in their soles.

Starting in 1977, this unique event was almost lost following the foot and mouth outbreak in 2002, when it stalled for a couple of years. However, Tempo Events, with the help of original Race Director David Joyce, got the thing up and running again from 2005. Richard's a handy bloke to have on board as he knows all the farms and landowners. A strict finishing time was adhered to and cut-off points are administered for those struggling (adding a sense of jeopardy).

There were generally two cut-off points. The first at around the 7-mile mark in Newchurch, at 90 minutes after the start, so if you reach this after that time you will be able to get a lift on to the finish. The second cut-off point will be at 10 miles in Gladestry, which from memory was a two hour cut-off. Back in my day it was a very popular event, with runners coming from all over the country to complete in this beautiful, but challenging race.

TIME: 2.04.00

Running Log

Event:	**Gloucester Carnival 7,**
Distance:	**10K**
Date:	**July**

Annual round-the-houses affair with the start and finish in the Park, with loops up and around Tuffley Avenue

TIME: 43.04

Runners line up in Gloucester Park

Robbo's run

TEWKESBURY Athletics Club's Graham 'Robbo' Robinson seems to specialise in runs which are away from normal road racing venues.

His latest effort has been the race between Hay-on-Wye and Kington which apart from short stretches of road near the two towns follows the Offa's Dyke footpath through some very spectacular countryside.

As well as the usual steep climbs and long up and down hill hazards this year's runners had to overcome very warm conditions.

Robbo's time of 2 hours 4 minutes was more than satisfactory and good enough to place him 289th out of more than 700 finishers.

Gloucestershire Echo

Running Log

Event:	**Glasgow Marathon**
Distance:	**26.2 miles**
Date:	**20th September**

Out of the all the Marathons I took part in, this was my most disappointing, both in time and performance. I had banked a solid year of training together with racing, with little injury to speak of. So I was looking to Glasgow to duck under the 3-hour barrier. The mistake I made was plumping for a holiday in the Highlands prior to race day. Having relaxed and chilled (not to mention over indulged during the trip), this wasn't conducive for a fast time, which I soon discovered come race day.

Although this was a race I was really looking forward to, worrying signs for the organisers were flashing as 'only' 5,516 started, this was a huge drop-off from previous years. A lack of TV coverage and the lack of a major sponsor for the event were cited as possible reasons.

In an effort to increase the quality and quantity of the field, the course was made easier and prize money was put on offer for the first time. However, these incentives did not make much of an impact, with again no TV coverage, and the prize of a car for anyone bettering 2hr 13mins, remained unclaimed.

Glasgow was selected as City of Culture the following year (1988), and for this race the race organisers did their level best to introduce the field to some stunning

Massed runners pass The Lighthouse on Mitchell Street.

Hutchesontown

Hutchesontown is a district that makes up part of the Gorbals in Glasgow's South Side. After decades of squalor and deprivation, it was earmarked for comprehensive development in the 1950s. The tenement slums were demolished to make way for exciting new high-rise developments. It was one of the most ambitious projects of its time. The daring initiative proved to be an expensive failure. The tower blocks were cheaply built and were deemed unsuitable for habitation in many cases. Most of Hutchesontown has seen continual regeneration since the late 1980s to reverse the damage caused by the ill-planned high rise estate, most notably by the Crown Street Regeneration Project. Most of the tower blocks have been demolished.

GLASGOW MARATHON
2327
NIKE **1987** **GLASGOW HERALD**

Victorian architecture. Leaving the major thoroughfare of Gallowgate, several Macintosh buildings were jogged past, including my favourite the 'Lighthouse', the imposing former water tower on the corner of Mitchell Street. The morning was damp (as ever in Glasgow), but light rain - although not welcome in the early miles - wasn't a problem. George Street, then past Glasgow Central and out along Sacuhiehall Street. We started to leave the city streets behind and move out towards leafier suburban roads. It was the loop out around the University and Kelvingrove Park where I ran into trouble. I'd past the 10-mile mark comfortably in 64.00. I think this spooked me. Instead of thinking 'just take it easy for the next couple of miles' I panicked, thinking I can't possibly keep this pace up and so I stopped running. The dread of having to run another sixteen miles just blew my mind. It was there in the next quarter of an hour or so that I blew my sub-3hr chance. I'd lost my focus somewhere up Ben Nevis!

Somehow I got going again and coincidently the rain stopped. The route crossed the

Clyde and took us on another loop, this time around the Gorbals. This was an area of Glasgow which was again going through a period of redevelopment. Back in the 1950s the tenements were all pulled down and the slums swept away, replaced by shiny hi-rise blocks of flats.

Now in the late 80s it was the turn of the flats to be demolished. Huge swathes of wasteland were left, some 3 square miles of bricks and rubble. This made running through the Isle of Dogs seem like a doddle, the landscape of boarded-up half pulled-down buildings did nothing to soak up the miles. The only amusing oddity I could take from this somewhat nuclear excursion, was that

Scott's Porage

MARATHON
THE SCOTTISH PEOPLES MARATHON
GLASGOW

GLASGOW

scale 1:40 000   north

R____Refreshment Stations   M__Medical Service   T____Toilets

between the strewn crumbling brick and dust that was on each corner somehow a pub had survived!

It is true my pace quickened through this deprived area. No one wants get caught in the Gorbals! Once more crossing the Clyde the field entered Glasgow Green, the oldest park in the city. Irritatingly for me and to make up the marathon distance, we had to run several loops of the park. I could see the finish gantry but I was marshalled in the opposite direction and past several of the park features; Doultons Fountain, McLenan Arch included, none of which I was interested in at that very second. Eventually I crossed the finished line.

TIME: 3.27.05

For the record, *the men's race was won by Dublin's Eamonn Tierney in 2.19.09, the slowest winning time in the race's history. A new name in the women's event was Scottish lass Sheila Catford, who threatened the course record, winning in 2.37.31, but finished less than half a minute off the best time. Second once more was Leslie Watson, again first women's veteran, competing in her 140th marathon. Third place went to Penny Rother of Edinburgh AC with a time of 2.54.27. This was the last year in which the race distance was the full 26 miles 385 yards. As sponsorship interest and promoting partners' interest faded, the Glasgow Marathon 1995 saw its peak of 11,492 finishers.*

Racing in the black and gold colours again. Where's my pint of heavy now?

Running Log

Event:	**Weston-super-Mare**
Distance:	**Valentines Day Massacre**
Date:	**14 February**

TIME: 1.31.00

Life's a beach - on my way to a promenade finish

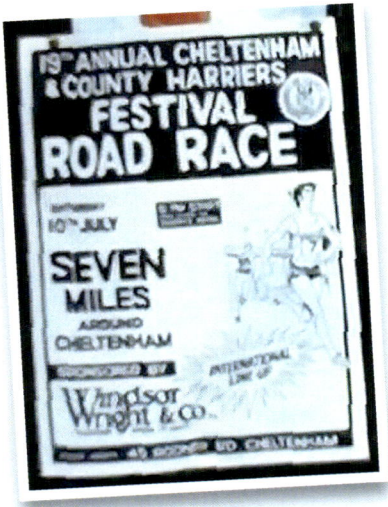

Running Log

Event:	**Wyedean 15 - 'The race that**
Distance:	**got away' - 15 miles**
Date:	**July**

Some years ago, while a guest at a Running Club's 25th Anniversary Dinner, my former team mates from Tewkesbury AC asked me to regale the 'Fleeting Victory' tale. As I'm a founding member of Tewkesbury Running Club (which was officially formed back in 1984 and unlike many other outfits in the area at that time didn't take itself too seriously). We were much more sociable than other clubs, and enjoyed a beer on club training nights and certainly post-race.

Turning out for Tewkesbury AC and donning the Black & Gold back in those days was a lot of fun. But, nevertheless, we took part in some serious club racing. Apart from local notables such as Steve Brown and Dave Catlow (Cheltenham Harriers), Norman Wilson (Bourton RR), Les Davies, Martin Daykin (Gloucester RC), the latter being a world record holder at Ultra Distance. Martin famously drank Newcastle Brown Ale, he overtook me once in the Gloucester Marathon nearing the conclusion munching a Mars bar and dressed as a can of brown ale! We also occasionally tested ourselves against international runners such as Nick Rose (Bristol AC), and Richard Nerurkar (Bingley Harriers).

My tale goes back to the hazy summer of 1988 when we had an abundance of evening race events to race at. Evening races were held throughout the summer, mainly short events, some you might remember?

The Cheltenham Festival 7 mile, a couple of laps of the town centre finishing outside the council offices behind Neptune's Fountain. **The Gloucester 7**, starting and finishing in the Park, which included the now infamous Cromwell Street as the finishing straight, and in through the Park gates. But perhaps the one I remember most is the **Lydney 6** which had an horrendous hill (if you've ever driven into Lydney, you will recall the steep descent into the town centre). We had to run up this twice with all the local populous in their front gardens jeering at us. Nice neighbourhood! The start and finish was from the Rugby ground. The other memorable event was the '**Beer Race**' raced over Minchinhampton Common. A short 4 mile course with a small can of Whitbread PA for all finishers. You can tell how long ago this all was!

As I say, mainly short distance events, however the one I'm going to tell you about is a 15 mile event. This was very unusual and had attracted a bumper field. Held in the Forest Of Dean it was very accessible for the Welsh running clubs of Chepstow, Les Croupiers and those beyond the Severn Bridge.

Five Acres School was where the race started from and it was called the **Wyedean 15**. It was a hot sticky evening, and at the race briefing we were told of a drinks station which was on the course and we would visit twice. The course was basically a run out into the forest, followed by two laps, and then a return to the finish. We all lined up. Bang! We were off, a lap of the playing field was completed before we filed out toward Berry Hill and a glimpse of the Rugby ground.

My pace had started to settle as the leaders were beginning to sort themselves out. *Pace myself, pace myself* was my mantra.

We eventually hit the everglades and, under the canopy of trees, the temperature was much better. Running in the forest is wonderful; soft and springy underfoot, with a carpet of needles and the fresh rarefied aroma of the pines. After about 2.5 miles the drinks station appeared.

I hastily grab the white ridged plastic cup from the camping table, and I squeezed most of the contents out, but thankfully I managed to drink the remainder and at least get my mouth moist. The Marshalls' and supporters' encouragement lifted the pace for a few hundred yards. On I went heading now toward English Bicknor. No other runners were overtaking me now, we seemed to have found our pace. Mile markers, though seemed to have disappeared or at least I hadn't seen one for twenty minutes or so. On I push, I can see runners up ahead. *Try and keep them in sight* I say (my mantra has changed).

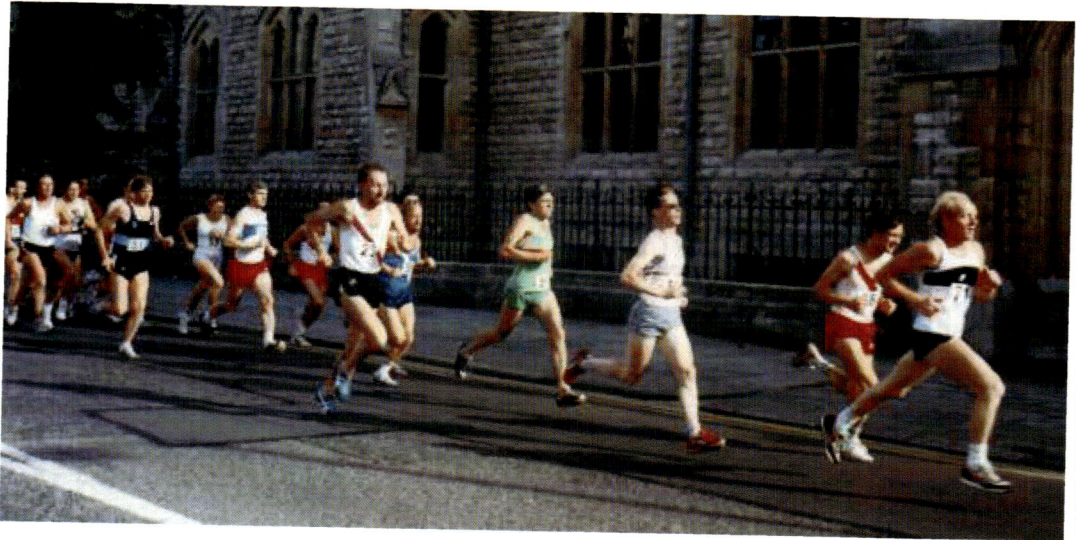

The Cheltenham Festival 7 mile

The Forest has a labyrinth of paths and routes running through it and it's very easy to get lost or lose track as one forest trail looks like another. Little twists of red and white plastic marker tape were tied to various branches, fences, or whatever was available to mark the route.

The race had now taken us out toward Shortstanding and we neared the end of the first lap. I set off on the second lap. It was familiar now and a comfort as I knew where I was going. The course had evidence of a few hundred runners, as grass and mud had been trampled. Marshalls cheered us on again for another uplifting few hundred yards.

I neared the end of the second lap. I was flying. I had 11 miles or so in the bag. I felt good except annoyingly I had lost sight of the runners ahead. Perhaps I was actually slowing and hadn't timed my finish correctly? *Don't let the doubt in Robo just keep it going* (the latest mantra).

Then it happened. I rounded the fire road bend to meet a shimmering heat haze. I could see the heat reflecting back off the white gravel track. Ahead was the Drinks Station (thank God). In my head it meant under 3 miles to go. As I approached the table and forest of white plastic cups the applause was of a more determined note. The Marshalls looked a little confused, surprised even and started checking their watches. But the 'keep it going' shouts from supporters and general encouragement was deafening. Somehow, I WAS LEADING THE RACE! If the race organisers on walkie-talkies were confused and in panic mode, how do you think I felt? How could this be, a Tewkesbury runner in front? I tried to clear my mind and forge on. From feeling in pretty good shape my legs suddenly felt like jelly.

It transpired that out in the forest at a particular junction the appointed Marshall had disappeared behind a forest pine to answer the call of nature. In doing so he had missed the leading group. Thus, the leaders missed the turn, taking dozens of runners off course with them. It was a mile or so before they realized and doubled back. Meanwhile, the said Marshall had resumed his station by the time I trundled by.

I was only 2 miles from home and I'm out on my own, leading the race - Ahh, the loneliness of the long-distance runner. I shouldn't have worried, I wasn't alone for long. Nevermind, the crowd of race followers had drifted down the course to offer encouragement to their club mates and loved ones. I received shouts and applause or so I thought. But you guessed it, I was being caught by the lead runners. I looked behind and a whole flurry of runners were in hot pursuit. Ahh, the agony of it, and by now I was back within sight of the school, and slowly one by one overtaken by the field. *Hang on to them Robo* (my now desperate mantra).

I lost count of the club vests which sped by me, and I'd certainly forgotten about the final loop around the perimeter of the playing field. God, it was agonizing, but I mustered a sprint towards the finish line. At least I hope that's what it looked like.

While the heated protestations took place over the cock-up, I headed for some shade and a cool pint in the New Inn (Shortstanding) beer garden. Final position: 54 / 215

TIME: 1.39.28

Running Log

Event:	**Singapore**
Distance:	**10k**
Date:	**1988**

For my participation in this exotic race I can thank my association to the Hash House Harriers, which inadvertently led me to this event. I was over in the Far East en-route to attend an Inter-Hash gathering taking place in Bali in Indonesia. And, along with my group of hashers, we had decided on a stop-off in Singapore.

The reason for my trip of a lifetime was to visit the hash homelands and two significant milestones. Most notably the Hash Hash Harriers Golden Jubilee in Kuala Lumpur, followed by the Inter-Hash in Bali. We stayed whilst in Singapore at the YMCA, a very upmarket version to what I'd experienced previously. An ideal location, just two minutes from the main thoroughfare of Scots and Orchard road.

Of course I went hashing while in town, the first of which was with the Singapore Harriers. The RV was from recently cleared scrub land. We registered for the event /hash (which is called a pre-lube) and after a quick rub down with insect repellent we were off. After about an hour of unfamiliar territory, unfamiliar markings and particular unfamiliar and evil-looking vegetation – we lost the trail! Our native hosts didn't seemed perturbed at all. They just waved down taxis and disappeared into the evening traffic. Meanwhile, the tourists keep at it and by chance found the Chinese Hare who took pity and showed us the route to the On-On (finish). This was down at the Marina, at the oldest Yacht Club in Singapore, which was quite a lavish affair laid on by the girls. A couple of nights later, on the Friday evening, we tried Lion City HHH. We had a cab ride across the city to find the RV (no mobiles or internet remember), it was all pretty vague and nail biting as we didn't know where we were going. Somehow

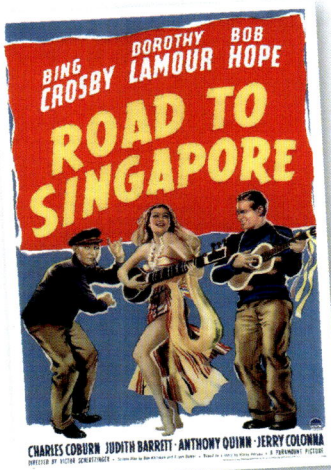

we found the site - an open air restaurant. The run was good and fairly long, but varied. With more hash visitors now in town, I was feeling more of the scene now. The run finished in darkness, only the occasional Kampon for guidance.

The Hash House Harriers had started in Asia - Malay to be precise - and was founded in Kuala Lumpur in 1938, predominantly by a chap named A.S. Gispert. 'G' was an Englishman abroad, working as an accountant in the rubber plantations in Malaysia. With the second world war raging in the Asian Rim 'G' volunteered and joined forces with the Federal Malay States Reserves, and found himself up on the Johor Bahru causeway (the southern end of Malaysia Peninsular), trying to fend off the Japanese. Sadly, in a rearguard action, whilst defending Singapore to the north of the island, he ran into mortar fire and was killed in action on the 15th February 1942, practically the last act of war before the British surrendered. This was up near the Causeway in the region of Bukit Timah (meaning Tin Hill), which is a hilltop area and a great position for an advancing army. Here is where G lost his life. Part of this region is a reserve, but also includes a race course, the Turf Club. Coincidently, during my stay that weekend a 10K race was being run in aid of the Olympic Games in Seoul.

The particular afternoon of the race coincided with a planned visit to Raffles. This famous Hotel which Stamford built on the beach (would you believe), is one of the 'to do' things when in Singapore. One to take in the splendour of British Colonial architecture, and of course to sip the renowned Singapore Sling cocktail. Much to my 1st wife's bewilderment and my Hash friends' amazement, I left them on the terrace in the shade and set off across the Island. It wasn't easy to get to - it took a bus ride and then a taxi up to the Turf Club on a sweltering tropical afternoon.

Hundreds had turned out for this fundraiser and promotional race, and even though a hubbub was all around, it still felt like a pilgrimage to me - to get somewhere close to where the founder of the Hash fell. The race was ran over and around the racecourse, an undulating cross country chase, where I got some curious looks from the locals as they overtook me. Crossing the finish line was a relief, to dive for some shade and the mountains of isotonic stacked up.

Prize-giving had already started and unbeknownst to me, and against the grandstand backdrop, an oldish guy was handing out medals and pre-publicity Seoul Olympic tee shirts. After the winners received plaudits and trophies it was my turn, yes really! Much to my surprise it seemed I was up for a prize as 'first European'. I presumed that perhaps it was a case of mistaken identity. Either way, not everyone has been awarded a medal and tee shirt by the (then) Olympic president, Juan Antonio Samaranch.

TIME: 43.05

This wasn't the end of my trip, and the next day was the overland train journey to Malaysia across the Johore Straits and on up through the steaming Jungle. Dense deep dark green vegetation and chocolate brown rivers which wound themselves in and out of rubber plantations all around us.

Only days later I found myself running through the middle of it all! On the Monday we had the chance to visit the hallowed Selangor Club where the hash formed in 1938, (the Hash House) and drank in the famous long bar. While most of it has been lost in recent times to road expansion, I was lucky to have visited back then and was able to take in the Colonial splendour of the surrounds, where we were able to sign up for the Petaling HHH 6th annual torch-lit run.

It was a long humid coach trip out of KL to the run site where we drank gallons of a product called 100+ - an isotonic drink - yes, beer would have to wait.

Meanwhile, we sat around waiting for it to get dark. I hadn't taken a torch, it being an impromptu decision, and the jungle was pitch black. I was pretty glad to escape unscathed and return to the floodlit complex for the evenings' entertainment and Anchor beer. This was just the curtain raiser, as the highlight of this exotic trip was the chance to 'hash with mother'. Hash trails were quite long compared to the hash runs back in the UK, with distances between 8–12k. And at that time (unsure how they mark trails today), the time-honoured use of newspaper, cut into 4in squares and scattered in piles. Most of our party got bitten by the mosquitoes, which was hardly surprising given the jungle we ran through, and streams we waded through, which had swollen due to rains. All the On-Ons were held at (mainly) open-air restaurants.

Bali-Hi

The following weekend we completed the trip by attending the Inter Hash in Indonesia, the paradise island of Bali. It was the 6th International gathering held at Nusa Dua. It was just like in the brochures, uncluttered beaches and terraced paddy fields. As usual, the runs were held over the weekend. Kuta is where we made our base, which is in the south of the isle. This was also where the daily cavalcade of Bemos (a popular method of public transportation in Indonesia, are smaller than buses and can carry up to 10-12 passengers), gathered to take the runners across the island to various running sites. They had NO coaches or buses in Bali, so a dozen or so Bemos whisked you along dusty country lanes with outriders tooting horns as we went. The trails were stunning (and sweltering), but some wonderful backdrops to go running through. On the Saturday I went to Bajar Hot springs, where we could 'cool' off after the hash, and Sunday it was the turn of Ubud Monkey Forest. All in all, some memorable runs in an exotic part of the world. It whet my appetite for more Hash overseas adventures.

Running Log

Event: **Cotswold Way**
Distance: **Relay Challenge**
Date: **5th June**

The Cotswold Way has existed as a promoted long distance walk for more than 30 years. But it wasn't until following many years of lobbying by the Ramblers Association and others, its' special qualities were recognised and in 1998 the government approved its development as a National Trail. The Cotswold Way was formally launched as a National Trail in May 2007.

Back in 1988 when one of my family received palliative care in the Sue Ryder Hospice, I wanted to give something back to the staff and home after they had given such wonderful care. I came up with the idea of a sponsored relay run along the length of The Cotswold Way. I was, back then, heavily involved with the local hash group Cheltenham & Cotswold. The length was roughly 100 miles, so I just divided it up into ten sections. Some had to run a little more, some a little less, depending on where a convenient hand-over stage could be found.

Running from south to north, the first leg was staged to go from Bath Abbey at 5.00am. Running in teams of three, for safety reasons, we were set to go – except one of the trio hadn't turned up! This meant that at the last minute I was the replacement runner. The route, although well marked these days with erected posts and way-marks, wasn't back then, and the three of us got lost several times. Eventually we started to climb out of Bath and into countryside where, after seven miles or so, we handed on the baton at Brockham End (Golf course).

Cheltenham & Cotswold

Hash House Harriers

The day unfolded without too many more dramas. It really was quite fun and as the day wore on a great spirit was felt amongst the runners AND their entourage. The final leg was my designated leg. Well, at least I had time to recover from my stint on leg 1. It was a ten-mile stretch which only really becomes enjoyable after one has scaled Fish Hill, the huge hill which overlooks Broadway.

The final calamity was at the finish, or rather not the finish! The support teams and entourage had unfurled the bunting and the time keepers were poised. Typical of the hash they had set up the finish outside the Lygon Arms. As I ran up the High Street, I was shouting "No no, at the church! The end of the trail is at the Church!" It looked like a Benny Hill sketch as they rolled up the bunting and chased me up the street around to the church.

Mad dash along 100 mile path

A MAD rush is on to see who can run the 100-mile Cots-wold Way in the quickets time.

The Cheltenham and Cotswold Hash House Harriers ran the first ever relay attempt ahead of opponents Yate and District Athletic Club.

Red-faced Yate Club hoped to be the first to complete the gruelling run, but they were left standing by the Har-riers who ran the path last weekend, in aid of the Sue Ryder Home in Leckhampton.

Now Yate will be vying with the harriers for the fastest time on June 18.

BEAUTY
Trailmaster 'Robo' Robinson of the Har-riers said: "The Cots-wold Way stretches for almost 100 miles along the escarpment of the western edge of the Cotswold hills from Chipping Campden in the north to Bath in the south.

"It is outstanding among the network of long distance foot-paths, if not for it's sheer beauty then perhaps it's variety of route.

"One moment, it dances through long forgotten sleepy ham-lets, and next passes a stately manor and a motorway junction!"

Leg 1	Bath - Brockham	7 miles	1.01.51
Leg 2	Brockham - Tormarton	9.5 miles	1.35.00
Leg 3	Tormarton - Alderley	11 miles	1.42.17
Leg 4	Alderley - Dursley	10.5 miles	1.31.12
Leg 5	Dursley - Standish Wood	11 miles	1.27.34
Leg 6	Standish Wood - Coopers Hill	10.5 miles	1.39.00
Leg 7	Coopers Hill - Severn Springs	10.5 miles	1.27.14
Leg 8	Severn Springs - Wontley Farm	10 miles	1.49.39
Leg 9	Wontley Farm - Stanton	11 miles	1.35.29
Leg 10	Stanton - Chipping Camden	10 miles	1.19.57
		Total time:	15.04.21

Running Log

Event: **Cheltenham 88**
Distance: **Half Marathon**
Date: **18 September**

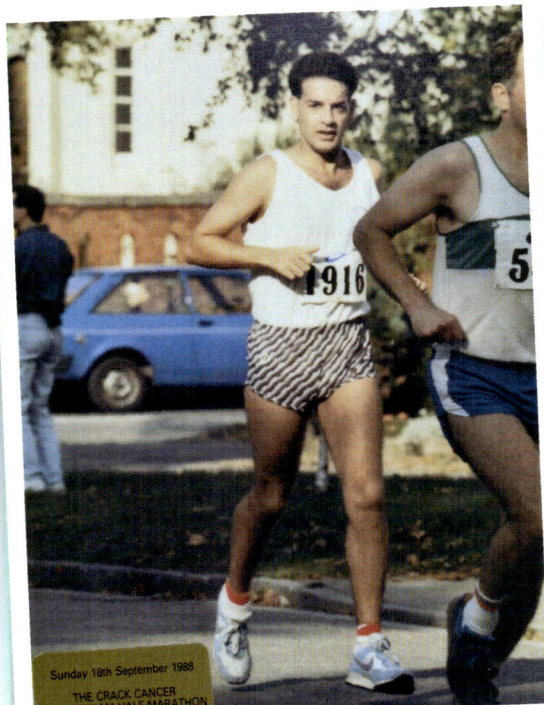

Sunday 18th September 1988
THE CRACK CANCER
CHELTENHAM HALF MARATHON

Coming in on the rails, just two furlongs from the racecourse

TIME: 1.41.09

Running Log

Event: **Badminton 88**
Distance: **(Horseless) Trails 8**
Date: **September**

This was another wheeze of an idea. A team event to run around the famous equestrian cross-country course minus the horse! It was the full course with most of the obstacles and fences to clamber over and the finish was across the lake in front of the house.

Again I'm unclear where I heard about this jolly jape, as none of my friends are in the horsey set. However, it appealed to me, and others. So one night after a hash run I managed to sign up enough to enter two teams of four for an unusual belt around Badminton. Held on the Duke of Beaufort estate, the all-terrain course takes the runners along country tracks and around the famous equestrian cross-country course. It ran for a full 9 miles taking in most of the jumps and obstacles with runners getting a 'leg up' over some of the fences.

The finish across the lake in front of Badminton House was a stand out moment - some had to swim for it - even though it cut across the shallow end. The dip was welcome after a warm run. The hash didn't win any honours, but was great fun and the reward was a pint on the route home.

TIME: 55.22

Running Log

Event:	**Kingswinford, Dudley**
Distance:	**10K**
Date:	**May**

This was (is) a traditional evening race based at Kingswinford RFC. Plenty of local supporters were out on the roadsides to cheer on a bumper entry. This was a very popular Midlands event, with many top local vests attending. I hadn't raced for a while and set off far too quick, covering the first mile in 6.25. The second wind eventually caught up with me and I finished in a group to record a PB. The real treat was after as we popped across towards Himley to visit the Crooked House pub for a couple of traditional Black Country ales.

TIME: 42.32 (PB)

Footnote: *Incredibly, during the process of penning this book, events connected to this cherished pub took a sinister twist. In the dead of night on the 5th August it was burnt down; Marstons had sold the pub to a private firm which just so happened to own the land-fill site behind the pub, and nine days after the sale, a suspected arson attack gutted it. Less than 48 hours later it was demolished without permission and prompted a national outcry. The Mayor of West Midlands, Andy Street, said "We have the bricks stored in containers, and they've been ordered to rebuild the pub back to what it was before the fire".*

Sometimes you can't make it up.

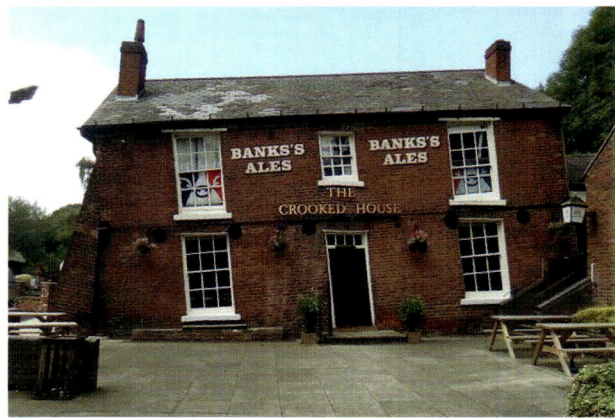

The gutted pub (Picture: PA Media)

Running Log

Event:	**Donnington Dawn to Dusk**
Distance:	**15 pubs**
Date:	

This was the second of a trio of charity fund raisers I organised. Donnington being a brewery and the route, mostly cross country, running from pub to pub (15 in total). The picture of me downing a pint of BB is starting off proceedings at seven in the morning from The Fox, Little Barrington (see P.36 for details of monies raised).

Running Log

Event:	**Icknield Way**
Distance:	**Half Marathon**
Date:	**May**

Running Log

Event:	**Bourton-on-the-Water 15**
Distance:	**15 mile**
Date:	**June**

Here was another multi-terrain event which fitted my new athletic focus. I began to enjoy the rugged nature of these races and the exploratory side of discovering somewhere new! This race was in its infancy The Icknield Way half marathon, which I believe these days is now refigured and ran as the Wendover Half Marathon, organised by Headingly Road Runners.

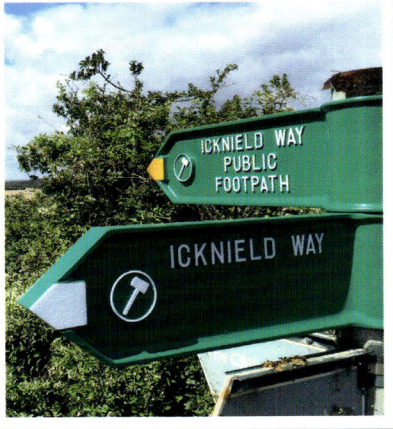

Claimed to be "the oldest road in Britain". Extending from the Dorset coast to Norfolk, the ancient route of the Icknield Way consists of prehistoric pathways, old even by the time the Romans came. Dotted with archaeological remains, it survives as splendid tracks and green lanes along the chalk 'spine' of England, laying in the shadow of the Chilterns.

These days it's a modern long distance footpath which stretches to 110 miles, so we only did small sections of it, starting and finishing in the village of Chinnor. The Icknield Way was named in the 1130s, and ranks along side with Ermine Street, Fosse Way, and Watling Street, as an important ancient English highway.

TIME: 1.37.53

is a real honey pot for visitors. Set deep in the Cotswold hills, it's a real tourist trap if ever there was one. The River Windrush, which runs through the village, adds to its quaint Olde English feel. The Americans and Japanese swarm around the place in the summer. It is also a good place for sports with thriving football and cricket teams, and of course a running club - Bourton Road Runners.

The Bourton 15 no longer exists. It is another lamented race that had become a real classic of the Cotswolds. If I remember correctly, it was held on a Saturday evening. As a quirky distance, it proved unpopular with the newly-established jogging clubs, as the 10K distance had become the norm. However, it has now been replaced by a Half Marathon entitled the 'Hilly Half', introduced in 2004 to replace the 15 mile race, which had been running for over 20 years.

In its heyday, the Bourton 15 was something of a draw for top runners, many of International class. On the particular evening I took part, a certain Richard Nerurkar was seen warming up and causing a stir amongst the local athletes.

The start line was just adjacent to 'Bird Land' on the edge of the village, the finish was much, much further into the heart of the village (I discovered much to my chagrin later). The course used the lane (Rissington Road) out of Bourton which eventually picked up the steep hill which jinked through the hamlet of Little Rissington, then gave you another steep climb to the top and the cross road. The course turned right and began a long climb. At least there was a flat stretch where, after the climb, you could try and get a second wind.

To the left of the competitors lay RAF Rissington. Here is where the Red Arrows gave their first Aerobatic display. They were initially based at nearby RAF Fairford, but it was here they first performed their world-wide renowned stunts. Whilst the air strips and occasional hangar still exist, the site was closed in 1994.

I had settled into a comfortable pace. The course took a right and starts to drop back down. Past the Cricket Ground on your left and just a bit further along there is a smashing 18th Century village pub, The Lamb. This popular country hostelry with a lovely garden is ideal to watch the race from on a sunny Saturday evening.

Picturesque Bourton-on-the-Water

Indeed, as I neared the pub, I heard a shout of encouragement which I wasn't expecting. Alan Cosford, himself a decent runner with Gloucester AC and regular runner with the hash was, along with his girlfriend cheering and holding up a pint. "Go on Robo, keep going – do you fancy a pint?" and laughed. I shouted "yeah okay" back over my shoulder, gave him the thumbs up and carried on my way.

It was along this stretch before the second loop where I sensed a commotion behind me. It was the leader gaining on me. Then it happened: Richard Nerurkar swept past me, International athlete or not, oh, the humiliation, I was lapped. So, nothing else for it - you just had to dig in and do that climb all over again.

The relief felt when getting to the top once more probably can't be beaten, or could it? Along the frontage of the Air Field once more and then at last turning right down the narrowing lane towards The Lamb. The cheers again could be heard in advance as runners were given plenty of encouragement. Here waiting was my personal reward and encouragement. Alan had indeed kept his promise. He presented me with a pint of beer at the side of the road. My goodness I enjoyed it, downed in three swigs. The pub garden audience once again erupted as I wobbled (and belched) on my way!

Down once more to the marshals on the corner, this time of course most insistent that the field turned left for the village of Bourton on the Water. We've all experienced that timed effort to the finish line, and the ones that go slightly awry. I had upped my pace as the village came into view. Not far I thought, except the finish wasn't where we started at Birdland. The gantry and finish was a further 800 yards or so in the main street. Great for spectators, not so good for a spent runner!

TIME: 1.52.06

The following year **Richard Nerurkar** represented Great Britain in the European Championships in Split, Yugoslavia (now Croatia). He finished fifth in the 10,000m. His first Marathon was in Hamburg in May 1993 where he won in a time of 2.10.57. In the fifth World Marathon later that year in San Sebastian (Spain), he led GB to a bronze medal where he won the race in a PB of 2.10.03.

Running Log

Event:	**Kingswinford, Dudley**
Distance:	**10K**
Date:	**Spring**

A return to this race to end a few seconds down on last year's efforts.

TIME: 42.37

Running Log

Event:	**Bath Hilly 10**
Distance:	**Claverton Down**
Date:	**June**

This was a race with its start and finish at Bath University up on Claverton Down. It was organised by Team Bath AC. I say was, because this is another race which has sadly bitten the dust through a lack of entries. In its final year (2015) it only had 42 entries, which meant staging the race just wasn't viable. It was never the fastest course – so PB's weren't high on the agenda. It consisted of a one-lap course on country roads through beautiful countryside. It was a great challenge and experience.

TIME: 1.06.00   Position 58/96

Running Log

Event:	**Birchfield Harriers**
Distance:	**10K**
Date:	**July**

A very fast and flat course around Perry Bar Park, on an incredibly sweltering July evening. But the real treat was the novel ¾ lap finish inside the Alexandria Stadium on the track. I even clocked up a PB!

TIME: 42.04 (PB)

On 17th April this year my first son Jared was born. As a teenager he went on to represent Cheltenham & County Harriers.

Running Log

Event:	**Offa's Dyke Charity Relay**
Distance:	**177 miles**
Date:	**24th-26th August**

PMW Michael Wallace writes…

We were sitting in the Crown & Harp in Bishops Cleeve, having held a committee meeting and deciding on policy for the Hash (C2H3) for the coming year, when Possidrive asked what would we be doing as a fund raiser to follow our Cotswold Way and Donnington Dawn to Dusk relay runs of previous years. Our GM went quiet and a bit misty eyed and finally admitted he had something in mind. But he's a thoroughly devious lad and it was weeks later he revealed his plans.

Since 100 miles of the Cotswold Hills had been such a doddle (ahem), how about 177 miles of Anglo -Welsh mountains? Now this idea should have been drowned at birth, I blame the Tetleys (we hadn't any), and anyhow by this time we were now in the Leckhampton Inn and Robo's maps and paperwork was strewn over 6 tables, 1 pool table and the bar. If you stood still for long enough you risked having your intimate parts measured for gradient. We were ON ON !

Next came the fun bit as we drew for lots for sections of the Dyke Path. The master plan was to run it over 2 days over the August Bank Holiday. The halfway mark being identified as Knighton, between Clun and Radnor Forest, as our stop-over on Saturday night. Having digested the prospect of the task, most of us settled down to gleaning information about our 'legs' But most, if not all the reading matter was out on loan at the public library, you beat me to it. We started to think about sussing our relay legs next, but thinking about it was as far as it went for a while. When we did get to grips with the task, we found that Robo hadn't exaggerated the difficulties. Long steep gradients, gut-wrenching tree and rock-strewn descents, and stiles you needed a step ladder for. [This post-run appreciation and description of how the challenge got off the drawing board highlights just what a feat this was].

Problems started to arise as arranging accommodation, sponsorship and support seemed insurmountable. Also almost every relay leg was taking longer than expected to run in practice. This was serious, as the timings meant we couldn't complete the run in the planned 2 days. Could we start on Friday evening? Which meant travelling up during the afternoon. Some couldn't time off week days, it was all so daunting. Then Robo got the wind up about the effect on our health of this mighty undertaking and recommended that all runners get clearance from their GP's. What had we taken on?!

Then just like in the movies it all started to come good. Possi conjured up some sponsorship from somewhere to cover costs, Robo calculated that on the day with adrenalin flowing we could just make the first leg from Prestatyn to Rhuallt, some 8 miles, before it got dark! [*What Mike doesn't mention in his opening piece is the fact that he forgot his trainers, and so on the seafront had to sheepishly admit this schoolboy error on such an important occasion. So after a quick game of Cinderella, it was my trusted trainers that fitted the bill which saw PMW flap his way along the seafront and onto the Dyke proper*].

And so it started, an epic journey for a hash group. The route was split into 24 stages over the 2/3 days completing 90 miles on the first full day and 80 on day two. All the stages were tough some very remote, remember this was the days before mobile phones became available. Stage 3 from Bodfari to the Gate Cafe at Clwyd was mountainous and the most dangerous. I insisted that the trio (always legs of three runners for safety) took with them emergency rations, space blanket, whistle etc. My leg on the first day was stage 7 from Llandegla to Oswestry racecourse, storming Chrirk Castle on route (9.5 miles 1hr 40) Over night was spent dossing down on Knighton Drill Hall sleeping bags on parquet flooring - not the most comfortable. The next morning we set off from the Offa's Dyke Heritage Centre at 6am for another 11 stages. My stage was out of Pandy some 7.5 miles to Lllantilo Crossenny and the handover at the Hostry Inn. (time 1hr.04).

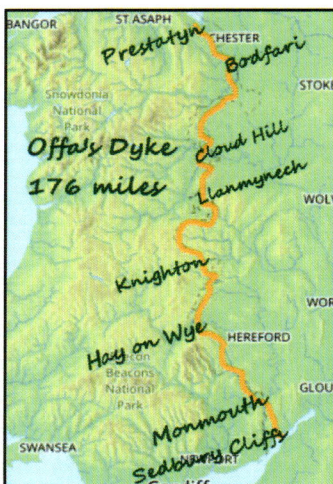

Relay runs are always eventful, whether it's over-zealous traffic wardens moving you on or the closure of public loos (just when you need one). Or even the realisation that high in the Black Mountains access from vehicles up to remote hand over spot would take 30 minutes on foot from Llanthony Priory. The timekeepers had to get a wriggle on and by sprinting the last 400 yards made the incoming trio and observed exchange.

The finish line is at Chepstow, rather a gloomy headland entitled Sedbury Cliffs. Back then it was even difficult to locate the actual pathway. I'm sure these days there's proper signage and insignia to mark the way. Nevertheless, it was a very emotional ending from a tremendous camaraderie had been forged over those three hard days of endurance (and fun).

COTSWOLD WAY - 5th JUNE 1988
- 100 miles • Time 15hrs 04.21
- Raised for Sue Ryder Hospice £1,450

DONNINGTON DAWN TO DUSK 9th July 1989
- 63 miles • Time 9hrs 22.05
- Raised for Magic Bullet Appeal £1,600

OFFA'S DYKE 24th 26th August 1990
- 177 miles • Raised for Multiple Sclerosis £2,800

Running Log

Event:	**Worcester Half**
Distance:	**Half Marathon**
Date:	**17th March**

Running Log

Event:	**Rhayader Round the Lakes**
Distance:	**20 miles**
Date:	**23rd March**

This was an event which popped up from nowhere. A one-off to commemorate the college centenary. My running diary states that the conditions were ideal, warm with a light drizzle. My race pace was also in check, starting steady in a 1st mile 7.50, with 10 miles at 75 minutes, enjoying a strong finish. The start and finishing areas were alongside the River Severn (Croft Road), ducking under the disused railway bridge for timing gantry and goodie bags.

TIME: 1.34.42

With the London marathon in mind, a trip to the Welsh Mountains seemed in order for some final preparation, and what has become a classic season opener. Off to the Welsh hills for a real classic race, both challenging and scenic. Starting in the quaint town square next to the clock tower. This seems to be a feature with Welsh races (*see Offa's Dyke*). The race took the runners on a downhill start out to the mountain road, where between 3–6 miles we had an 800-foot climb, followed by steep drop-offs, so the quads were screaming. I passed the 7 miles on the hour mark and went just over two hours (2hr 02) for fifteen miles.

The Elan Valley is a beautiful place to run around with water and mountains everywhere. There are six lakes which make up the reservoirs, most of which I ran round as well as crossing some spectacular Dams (Craig Goch and Pen y Garreg). After crossing the final dam you bear right and head back down the mountain pass, back to the town of Rhayader. This was a long drawn-out road back towards the town which took its toll, especially the uphill and subsequent dogged sprint into the cattle market finishing area.

TIME: 2.45.54

Running Log

Event: Cleevewold 14
Distance: Cleeve Hill
Date: March

This off-road event was only in its' second year, with the start and finish being at the Cleeve Hill Golf Club. Subsequent races now start from Postlip (further on around the hill). This day the Cleevewold was held in awful conditions. Hail, wind and freezing rain, not necessarily in that order! It's a tough endurance event with the lead-out beginning up the Cotswold Way toward the Pylons. The route covered the highest points of the Cotswold hills, zigzaging across Cleeve Common, before heading into the surrounding countryside, before returning via the Belas Knap (neolithic burial mound) and the abandoned Farm at Wontly.

I was glad to finish and get out of the exposed hill parts. Home for a luxury soak in a hot bubble bath.

TIME: 1.58.02
Position: 61/ 121

FOR THE RECORD
After his triumph at the inaugural race, Perry Somers (RAF Locking), came back and won the second year too, in a time of 1.29.02, 3 minutes down on last year (I said conditions were tough).

Running Log

Event: ADT LONDON MARATHON
Distance: 26.2 miles
Date: 21st April

It was some eight years later that I returned to the fray for another bash at the London Marathon. The sponsor had changed, now it was known as the ADT London Marathon, and had been in the middle of a four-year deal (1989-1992). Excitingly, London was chosen to host the newly-formed IAAF World Marathon Cup, a Nations' team event which started in Hiroshima in April 1985. This competition was staged every odd year.

Since my baptism back in 1983, my times had improved in other marathon races, and therefore I fell into a category which was looking for runners to run sub 3hr 15min. Brasher and Disney were keen to get their course a reputation for fast times. A fast course equals more entries, the security of the event, more prestige and world class field, etc, etc. It wasn't 100% guaranteed, but it wasn't a lottery either, and more often than not I got an entry based my personal best time.

For the 1991 event I had decided to stay in the Youth Hostel in Holland Park, not too far off the centre of London for the early start, and the logistics of getting to the start. Ah, the logistics of the start. After my first London marathon, I had decided to tone down the day-before activities, to give myself the best chance of a decent run and time. I attended the pasta party around tea time and then sloped back to the youth hostel (or rather a handy pub around the corner - The Castle, Holland Park Avenue).

An uneventful night meant I had a good night's sleep and was up and ready for the short commute into central London. It was another damp overcast morning and not very appealing, certainly not to be hanging about at the windswept start. I parked my van in a side street, tucked up behind St Martins in the Field, taking with me all I needed for the journey in my London marathon-provided kit bag. Going solo (you have to travel light), I set off for Charing Cross Station.

My plan was to catch the last train out to the start (Greenwich) which would mean not too long to hang around. While not quite a veteran of London Marathons, it was all still exciting, and I wanted enough time to have a loo visit, warm up and enjoy the throng and soak up some of the atmosphere not just the rain (yes, it had started to pour down. Oh good!) The platform was rammed and it seems everyone else had the same plan and was on 'my train'. I couldn't get on! What was I going to do now? As this was the last train to Greenwich, the only option was to catch the Blackheath train, but of course my start was at Greenwich. This was doing nothing for the tension and butterflies in my stomach. The train trundled into Blackheath station and the mass of runners, with the overpowering smell of wintergreen, wafted up the platform and onto the heath.

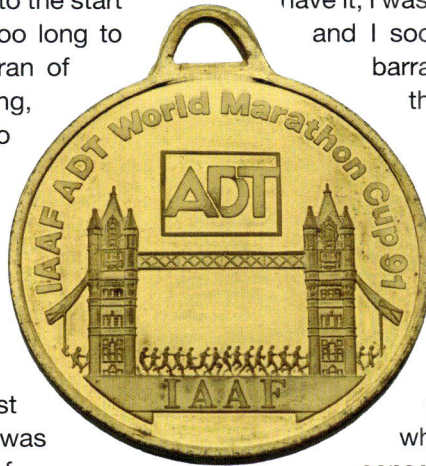

Blackheath is bracing at any time of the year, as this exposed expanse of green is pitched up at the elements. Once upon a time it was a wild heath with tangles of gorse and bracken and huge pockets and craters, most of which were in-filled after WW2 with blitz rubble, resulting from the Luftwaffe raids.

So while most, if not all of the runners turn right out of the station to go to their start, I turned left and had to work out roughly where Greenwich and my start was! A couple of road signs indicated where Greenwich Observatory was and So I set off in a steady jog in the general direction. As luck would have it, I was heading in the right direction, and I soon spotted a marathon start barrage balloon floating high in the grey sky which confirmed it. It wasn't too far to jog, but in truth it added an extra mile and a half to the twenty-six I was already contemplating. This was an anxious start to my big day. A huge shot of adrenalin wasted on just getting to the start area, where I really needed to conserve it for the race.

Bag stowed on lorry marked R, time now to don the bin liner and wait for starter's orders.

Being a 'World Cup' event, it certainly added an extra edge to your race against the distance. I was never going to make it to world finals at football. But somehow, although a dozen or so pens back from the elite field, it was like you were on the football pitch alongside Alan Shearer or Thierry Henry. It was still a tough run however, I guess 26 miles is never easy.

Splits: Tower Bridge 1.42.00, 20 miles: 2.36.34.

In the mass race, around 79,000 people applied to enter the race, of which 33,485 had their applications accepted, and around 24,500 started the race. A total of 23,435 runners finished the race.

TIME: 3.27.12

FOR THE RECORD

The individual race was won by Soviet athlete Yakov Tolstikov in a time of 2:09:17, and the women's race was won by Portugal's Rosa Mota in 2:26:14.

Tolstikov was relatively unknown, but he stole the show as he made his break at the 14-mile mark. He never lost the lead again and, in the process, recording a personal best. Although Tolstikov's run was a USSR (Soviet) record it never had chance to stand the test, as the country collapsed at the end of 1991.

This was the first time IAAF/ADT World Marathon Cup Championship had been incorporated with a mass participation, big money Marathon. The result was one of the finest in-depth fields ever assembled for a marathon outside a major championship.

Incidentally GB won the team event - (decided on total aggregate times)

Dave Long	2.10.30	4th
Steve Brace	2.11.45	7th
David Buzza	2.12.37	16th

London Spotlight - Going to the dogs

The Marathon route around the Isle of Dogs

The name Isle of Dogs conjures up all sorts of fanciful images and tales, of long-lost forgotten byways and waterways. It is, or rather was, an area relatively unknown to the wider population, even Londoners. That is until the London Marathon arrived.

Now every year the area gets a pounding - literally - as thousands of runners pass through this ancient corner of the capital, and receives national and international interest due to its role in the London Marathon. Many more thousands of spectators will be lining the streets. However, this is a huge contrast to the early days of the Marathon in the 1980s, when the Isle of Dogs suffered from transport problems and spectators generally watched the race start in Greenwich, and the finish in Central London. With no underground links to the Isle of Dogs (and the DLR not reaching Canary Wharf until 1991), for spectators it was impossible to get to. Any support was from local people, more out of curiosity, especially if enjoying a pint at the local. It was a working area and the population of the Isle of Dogs was a great deal smaller than today.

During the 1980s and 90s, race organisers had to contend with the massive building projects in and around Canary Wharf and often had to make small adjustments to the course, as much of the course went though dilapidated dockyards and warehousing. For most runners the narrow streets and the winding part of the course in the Isle of Dogs was at the 14–21 miles point, and had always been a challenge. A number of runners hit the invisible wall at this stage and struggled to complete the course. The biggest change besides the landscape was made in 2005 when the organisers decided to go anti-clockwise around the 'Island'.

Marathon running is thirsty work

Down in the Isle of Dogs many dockers pubs were available for a swift pint. Here's a guy emerging from the Queens pub at the top and junction of East Ferry Road and Manchester Road.

Then and Now

The pub was built in 1855 and its last landlords were Allied Breweries. Initially called the Queen, and then the Queen of the Isle from 1995. Of course, with the sweeping changes to the old East End, many of the landmarks (pubs) have been demolished. The pub in question was part of the regeneration and replaced by a supermarket in 2004.

Why the isle of Dogs?

It is thought that the Isle of Dogs' name originated in the 16th century. Some say that the name was given to the area because of the number of dead dogs that washed up on its banks. Others think that the modern name is a variation of other names. Given that the area was mainly marsh and swamp, it coined phrases such as the Isle of Dykes or the Isle of Ducks.

"Oh, that's better ladies"

Queen of the Isle (then)   (now)   Photos: Mike Seaborne

London Marathon at Free Trade Wharf - 1982 Race The litter is paper cups as there was a drink station a few gulps back.

Before and After
The white ornate gateway on the left and immediately flanking buildings, are all that now remain of the Free Trade Wharf buildings after redevelopment. However, the gateway (although changed beyond recognition and has become arched), is all that really remains. St Paul's Church spire (Shadwell) can be seen in the distance. Located near the Highway on the edge of Wapping. Evidence of the remaining entrance to the old Free Trade Wharf. Now a pedestrian entrance to apartments.

The public toilets on Manchester Road, (formerly next to the railway arches) were built in 1925 and were well known to Islanders, and lots of London Marathon runners. These shots are from the Mars sponsored 1984 race. The public conveniences became shabby and were closed and noted as an eyesore. However, when developers began to circle with rumours that the toilets were about to

be sold, demolished or redeveloped in some way, Islanders began to voice their concerns at the loss of 'their toilets'. Maybe it was the final straw that the people from the Isle of Dogs (Islanders) wanted something to remain. Even though they were pretty grotty loos, it was the principle. Over the last 30 years, Islanders had seen so much of the Island demolished and redeveloped - and so many new buildings constructed - that it has become imperative to fight for every last remaining square inch, before nothing remained.

Although a heavily industrialised area (once), it didn't matter for true Islanders, as although drab and unattractive, it was a reminder of how life had been, and how it was once home. Attempts were even made in 2012 to get the toilet building listed, in order to protect it. But English Heritage did not consider that there was anything special about the building that it should be preserved. It is still there however, with the nearest DLR station Island Gardens.

Cheque Presentation Evening at
The Victory Club, Cheltenham.

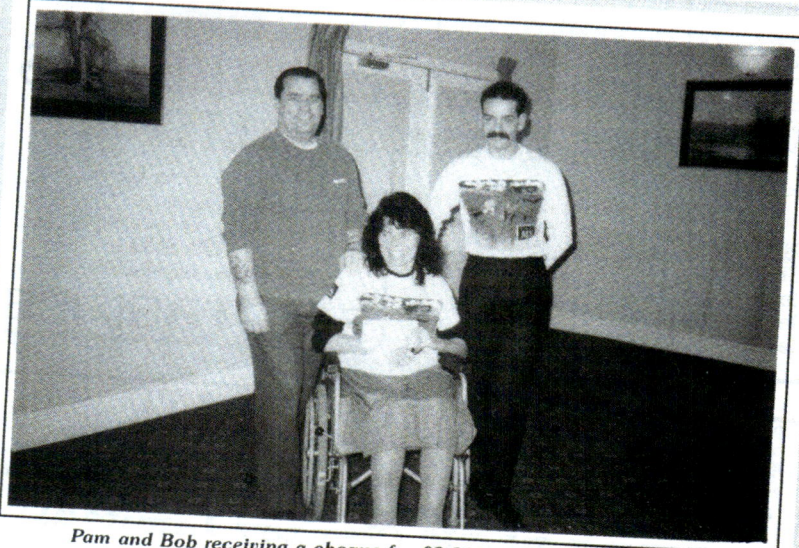

Pam and Bob receiving a cheque for £2,800 from the Grand Master
of the Cheltenham & Cotswold Hash House Harriers

Members of the Cheltenham & Cotswold Hash House Harriers

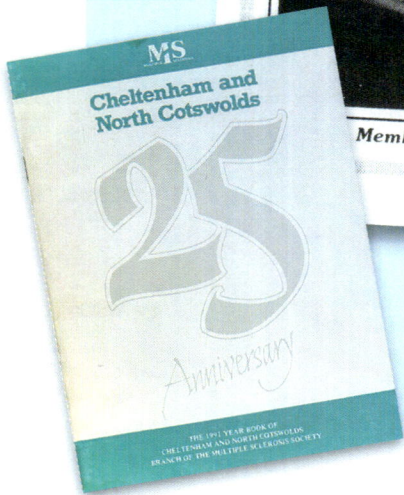

From the Multiple Sclerosis Society
25th Anniversary Magazine 1991

Running Log

Event:	**Whitbread Reading**
Distance:	**Half Marathon**
Date:	**26th April**

This race, which started in the early 1980s grew in popularity, as it was originally pitched in March as an ideal 'warm up' for the London Marathon. In the early days its' start and finish (and indeed changing facilities) were staged at the Rivermead Sports Centre, which is on the banks of the River Thames. Its initial sponsor was 'Sweatshop', one of the early specialist running shops back then - its proprietor no other than Chris Brasher (it's that man again).

The race started well enough with the field funnelling over the road bridge and heading into the town centre. The pace settled down and the odd conversation was struck up. However, things took on a different twist at mile 2! literally. Those who had studied the course map or indeed those who had competed the previous year said we're going the wrong way! A hastily rerouted course had taken place with marshalls shouting and gesticulating which street to run up. This diversion was mystifying as about 1.5 miles later (or so) we were shown back on to the 'proper course'. As the race settled back into its rhythm and we stopped shaking our heads, us runners were looking out for the next mile mark to check our pace. The next marker was the 6-mile board, which brought about a little panic or delight at the fast pace we were all charging along at. Of course, the mile markers were now obsolete as we found out the reason behind our diversion was a bomb scare.

Hard to imagine now, certainly since the Good Friday Agreement signed in Belfast in 1998 or to those of a youthful disposition. With the 'Troubles' in Northern Ireland, a persistent daily occurrence. Here on the mainland constant vigilance was needed as the IRA wreaked havoc with bombs 'planted' at railway stations and shopping centres. A car 'bomb' was often the weapon of choice which could be parked near a specific target area, a hoax phone call was enough to disrupt daily life, sadly it often wasn't a hoax.

It transpired that a van had been parked directly outside an Army Recruitment Office. The street had been race cleared and this motor vehicle 'just appeared' overnight. When the police couldn't raise the vehicle owner the bomb squad were called in. The police had cordoned off the streets surrounding the possible bomb site, and rather stoically the race organisers had sent us around and well out of reach of any impending explosion.

Anyway, back on the course, well after the ten-mile mark and on the run back to Rivermead, race timings and negative splits had gone out of the window. It was with mixed emotions we crossed the finish line and collected our medals. We were all pleased we didn't get blown up, but of course any personal bests were shattered as the course, even with the best efforts of the race organisers, had left the race distance short by some 700 metres.

> **FOR THE RECORD**
> Steve Brace won the race and completed a hat-trick, but of course his time of 62.19 is omitted from the record books.

Running Log

Event: **Evesham**
Distance: **Half Marathon**
Date: **Bank Holiday Monday May 5th**

Starting and finishing on Corporation Meadow, this was an ideal route to take in the Vales famous 'blossom' trail. The route soon leaves the town over the 'new bridge' and along Abbey Road before Cheltenham Road, turning sharp left to run parallel with the River Avon. The course then heads out into the market garden countryside, (well, at least it's a flat course). The incident of the morning which has gone into folklore, and for race organisers on what not to do.

After a fairly uninteresting stretch (main roads) we veered left at the Round of Gras (public house), so named after the term used to bunch asparagus. The race was heading out towards the Littletons, but first had to cross the level crossing at Blackminster. This was around the 6 mile mark and the race had settled with the leading group of runners strung out in front. There is a small kink in the road slightly downhill before the road rises up to the unmanned level crossing.

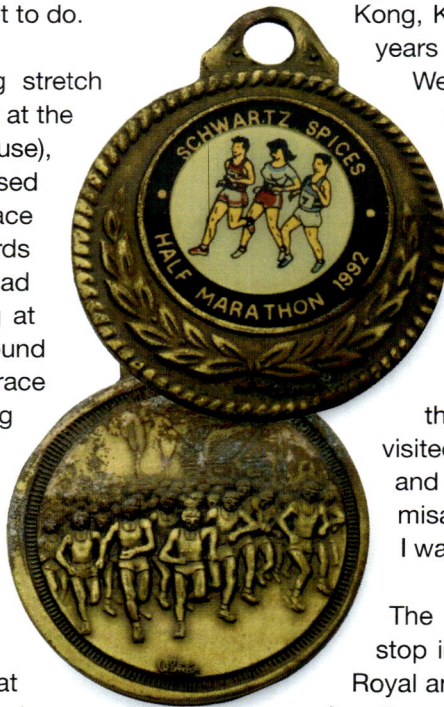

Arriving at the kink, that unmistakable warning noise started to emit. Then the flashing lights and - you guessed it - down came the barriers, allowing some 30-50 runners across the rail track. This left the rest of the field to bunch up against the barriers unable to cross as agonising minutes ticked by. Do we restart our watches? Some were tempted to sprint for it. Others just ran on the spot. What a cock up! It was rerouted the following year.

TIME: 1.34.16

Running Log

Event: **Inter Hash, Phuket, Thailand**
Distance: **Varied**
Date: **3/5 July**

The first invitational gathering of Hash House Harriers clubs was the 1000th running of Kuala Lumpur hash in March 1966. It wasn't until 1978 when the emergence of hash groups started to grow around the far east. Kowloon H3 thought they might host a major event (jokingly referred to as 'The International Hash Unconvention'). By May of 1977, invitations had been sent out. Based on the success of this gathering in Hong Kong, KL H3 stepped up to host again in two years time 1980. So the pattern was set. We now have World Inter hash every two years dotted around the Globe. It's been to these shores just once, held in Cardiff at the Millennium Stadium in 2004 (the 2026 event is to be held in Prambanan Menut in Indonesia).

I had now been hashing for over a decade and had started to really immerse myself into the origins and the folklore of the hashing world. Having visited the home of hash in Kuala Lumpur and written about it earlier in this tome of misadventures. So with sandals and socks I was once more off to the mystic Orient.

The trip to Phuket was preceded by a stop in Hong Kong where I hashed with the Royal and Ancient at the Monday hash, before heading onto Bangkok where, after a protracted hot and sweaty bus ride, turned out with the Bangkok Harriers.

Rather than go out on the trails I ran on the Isle of Smiles. I can tell you about a rather stand-out moment which happened quite by chance.

Situated on the east of the Island Patong Beach has rather sleazy reputation these days, and while it had its fair share of parlours and girly bars back then, it still had a modicum of decorum if you looked hard enough.

Phuket Tinmen H3
1st July 1992
Kan Eang Seafood Restaurant

As a pre-lube I turned out with the Phuket Tinmen, a Men Only Hash, which operated once a month on a Wednesday nearest to the Full Moon. The evening started as a nerve-shredding open-sided coach ride at top speed along dusty narrow back waters with blind bends thrown in for good measure. I was shaking when we finally alighted in the middle of nowhere.

This was a torchlight trail, so while we waited for it to get dark we helped ourselves to a beer from the beer truck. The Hares didn't really take any chances and it was a fairly tame run in the dark, just the odd Kampong which brought interest. The A-B route lasted only 30 mins or so and ended at a beachside restaurant on the shores of Chalong Bay.

Phuket H3 Run 325
2nd July 1992
Katu Valley, Bangatt Dam

The 120 Bhat registration fee got you a headband, and this it turned out, was a vital piece of running kit!. It was your ticket to board one of the assembled buses to get you to the run site.

This was central Phuket Island and away from the slight coastal breeze. From the first check you could tell it was going to be one of 'those' runs! The huge pack spread everywhere and found the out trail, false trails, and of course the in trail. A cascade of hash horns, whistles and On On calls had the pack running up and down. We then ran a complete circle starting and finishing on a little road. The pack splintered and some made for the coconut palms as we ran a loop twice and rounded Pineapple Hill (twice). I finally staggered back to the beer truck after finishing by running up a road (off trail of course), after 45 mins!

As is often the case the worse the hash, the better the circle. It was lengthy, but at least entertaining.

CIRCLES
Most hash runs, especially the milestone events, end with a group gathering known as a 'circle'. Here a Grand Master or Religious Advisor oversees the proceedings to recognize individuals, formally name members, or inform the group of pertinent news or upcoming events. However it's mainly to sing bawdy drinking songs.

Welcome Party
3rd July 1992

The Grand Opening night was a lavish gala, laid on for the Friday to open Inter Hash proper. The setting was the impressive Patong Resort Hotel, just one of the many state-of-the-art complexes to have sprung up.

The layout was impressive and to see such an array of hashers in such a backdrop added to the anticipation. The open air courtyard boasted 2 mouth-watering food areas with 3 beer bars interspersed. Two flights of stairs gave more room at each level in the form of large open verandas, complete with bars of course. On the grassy areas marques were scattered around in case of inclement weather. The stage was impressive and very big, although the dance area suffered as it was sandwiched between the stage and pool.

Welcoming speeches were kept brief and were received with a modicum of patience with the highlight being the introduction of Simon Gispert.

Simon, the long lost grandson of G, was stumbled on by accident by Howard McKay (a hasher of 2 Dogs Wranchai H3), who employed him in Hong Kong - there's not many with that surname.

Suddenly the lights dipped and a fireworks display lit up.

I mentioned a pool, and this of course was screaming for attention. Surprisingly, hashers remained nonchalant of the inviting waters - well, for an hour or two. When the first hasher went for a dip, security guards were in attendance and there followed a shriek of whistles and high-pitched incomprehensible Thai. The first offender was pulled out of the shallow end. Moments later, law & order broke down and the first of the security guards went in, at the deep end. Crikey! Hope he can swim! As the brown uniformed Thai sank without trace up popped his peaked cap and floated away on the ripples.

Consumption of Singha Gold was high, as was the quality of Thai cuisine on offer, well up to Master Chef standard. Queues were inevitable, but most took it with good humour. That turned a little sour as the grog was turned off at 11pm. Not another bottle of Singha was topped and someone pulled the plug on the 60s music (so it wasn't all bad). Most people had just gotten in the party stride, perhaps Phuket H3 had fears someone might drown.

Saturday

The runs were pitched for 1pm and came with an information leaflet, which took some deciphering for connection points and run sites. However, it all mattered not a jot, as a lack of buses and a complicated bye-law meant very few buses turned up, and then that meant a 3-hour wait. Luckily the long run queue was minimal and I was able to board a bus after an hours' wait.

'Lager site D', no other reference was given. What with all the beauty of this paradise Island, we were tipped off at a disused quarry. As a hundred or so hashers ran off along this approach road it was definitely policy to be front running as clouds of dust rose into the air and choked the back markers.

Over an open ditch - leaping to avoid any lurking snakes - followed at last by some pleasant shaded running, before running through razor sharp pineapple. Forget brambles, this stuff is lethal.

At the briefing we were reminded that the trail is marked in the traditional way, with paper (this was some 30 years ago), but it just seemed out of place littering this idyllic setting. A little further on, when emerging out of dense tropical vegetation into a clearing for a check, I took a breather and looked up from the pile of paper markings across to a palm covered hilltop, resting against a clear blue sky, and at that moment it seemed the most natural thing in the world.

The hash was laid by two Brits, a couple of Cambridge hashers who I knew, and what a good trail it was. Just on the hour (always the aim for a decent length trail), and running into the bowels of the quarry to find the beer truck.

Inter Hash Party Night

The entertainment was held in down town Phuket at the football ground, which I'm guessing saw its biggest attendance of the season. A mixed evening of dodgy cabaret acts and lewd singing was the usual fare, but the food and plentiful supply of Singha had no complainers. The evening ended a little abruptly and prematurely as the floodlights were doused to herald another firework display. However as it ended the hash crowd thought it was the finale and headed for the exits and the waiting coaches back to Patong. Of course what someone hadn't realised in the meticulous planning was that halogen lights needed fifteen minutes or so to cool down before being switched back on again. All that food and booze and an empty stadium!

Foot note from Phuket – Interhash 1992
Brief Encounter

As with most Inter Hash events, an up-market swanky hotel is used for registration and often opening ceremonies, entertainments and those excitable reunions. This was held at the impressive Patong Resort for such an occasion, much to my astonishment, the Island had a Holiday Inn. It seems I was behind the times and Phuket had been opened up to commercialism long before I'd even heard of it.

In 1976 Phuket airport became Phuket International, and onwards into the 1980s visitor numbers rose significantly, and with it construction of salubrious and brand-named hotels began to appear. The Holiday Inn Resort opened in July of 1987 at the rapidly developing resort of Patong. Anyhow, as the afternoon registrations wore on, in the palatial grounds of the Patong Resort, I noticed a small hubbub and gathering of hashers. In the midst of this mild-mannered scrum was a tall and frail elderly gent. As I approached I could easily recognise that it was none other than **Horse Thomson**. Yes, the last remaining member of the original founders - **Hash Royalty!**

So instead for heading for the free grog, I decided to wait my turn, and it seemed to take an age to get to meet him. In truth it wasn't much of a conversation it must be said, a mere handshake and nod of approval and how-nice-to-meet-you type vibe. But all these years on how significant my brief meeting was. To actually shake hands with a founder of the hash movement, one of the

A grimace from 'Horse' as he poses with a 'Sheila' and Aussie hashers

original famous four we always refer to, Gispert, Bennett, Lee, and Horse Thomson. I didn't realise at the time the significance of this chance meeting. Now of course I realise just how fortunate I was to be in the right place at the right time.

Following the Golden Jubilee celebrations in Kuala Lumpur I become a student of hash as I obtained a copy of the book that 'Magic' produced and became absorbed in the fascinating history. The excerpts can be largely attributed to his research and contributions from such luminaries as the late John Duncan On Sec of KL H3.

Horse was recorded as participating on the first run with the newly formed Hash House Harriers, and is listed as one of the first Joint Masters from 1938 (the founding date in 1938 has been disputed by Torch Bennett, as being in the summer of 1939) to 1940, and then again after the war in 1951 before his eventual departure from Kuala Lumpur.

Various accounts state that Horse was first allowed to leave Malaya before the outbreak of hostilities on the peninsula, and subsequently joined the Royal Air Force (RAF), who posted him to Hong Kong. Unfortunately, Japan launched an assault on Hong Kong the same day (8 Dec 1941), then it began occupying Malaya. Horse was taken as a POW, but after a period of time managed to escape. Teaming up with other rogue forces, they were recaptured, and Horse was shot in the neck during the encounter. He was returned back to Hong Kong where he recuperated from his injuries, but it left his head with a slight lean. This is possibly the reason that Horse was often seen with towel wrapped around his neck tucked into a tee shirt.

He was released after the war, and returned to Kuala Lumpur to resume his civilian life. He also rejoined the hash in 1946, when Torch got things going again. Like most of the other founding members, Horse was a British ex pat working in SE Asia as a manager at a Malayan telecommunications, which back then in the 1920s & 30s was telephone and anyone remember telegraph?

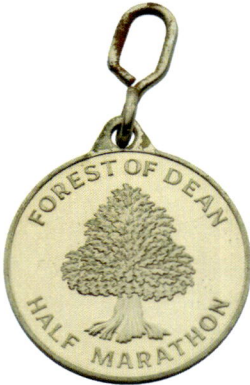

Lost Training Diaries

Following a spate of life on the road race scene over the next couple of years, the activity was toned down somewhat. I suspect the proud task of being a father curtailed my training runs. Indeed, I can't find any of my training diaries from a two- or even three- year period.

The 1991 to 1994 period also coincides with my involvement in organising the UK's National Hash Weekend (Nash Hash), held in August 1993. This was a particularly intense period with logistical headaches, and the glad-handing and promotional groundwork across the country left little time for training or racing.

Being the then Chairman (Grand Master) of Cheltenham & Cotswold HHH, it was quite a responsibility, but I had great support from family and friends, and we pulled off a magnificent weekend of trail running (hashing) and partying. We managed to entertain 750 over the August Bank Holiday when we borrowed Rendcomb College for the serious knees-up.

However, I did keep at it and managed a half marathon or two.

Running Log

Event:	**Warwick Castle To Castle**
Distance:	**10K**
Date:	**June**

I'm unsure why I entered this event, judging from my training diary. I suspect it was the novel event of racing from and to the magnificent backdrops of both castles – Warwick and Kenilworth. Starting in the grounds of Warwick Castle the route, was unfortunately most uninteresting. 'Boring course' I have noted, also it was a blistering hot day. The consolation was I improved my 10K time. 56 / 340

```
TIME: 41.27 (PB)
```

HARE AND HOUNDS
HARPER'S WEEKLY

May 23. 1874 l

44 l

Lost Up West - Hashing

Another excursion to the delights of West London to join the hash for their regular Thursday night run. No real dramas involving the Tube this time, although we cut it fine for the start as the train rolled into Gunnersbury. So we rushed up the escalator and onto the concourse where various hashers had already assembled.

Unbeknownst to us, tonight's hash was an A–B run with a black cab running on the meter already stuffed with hasher's bags. The Hares instruction was loud and clear "get your bag in the cab, collect at the end". Suddenly the Hash circle (briefing) was in full flow and as I looked over my shoulder the taxi screeched off.

Then the hash pack shot off, into the darkness and neon of London. We were On On. All started well if not at a phrenetic pace. With the pace settling down the out of townies (i.e. me), started to check out. This bravado caught two of us out as a hashing friend and I ran a false trail, only to return to the check point to find it deserted. Where was everyone?

Then of course that panic and realisation that we didn't know where we were, this residential backwater looked very much like the last one we ran down. A split second later it dawned on us that we also didn't know where we were heading to. The 'B' pub wasn't revealed at the Hares' Brief. We couldn't even ask the way. The jeopardy was heightened more when we realised all our worldly goods were in the back of a black cab heading somewhere in West London. So, no wallet, no car keys etc. change of pants, etc.

Pulling ourselves together from being gibbering wrecks, (think Jones, Dad's Army) we set off and dutifully followed the trail, but it wasn't always that clear. What was clear we had to run like billio, sussing out every check point and false trail as we went.

Adrenalin was coursing through our veins and mercifully and slowly we did catch the pack. Never before have I been so relieved to see the back markers. We never ran another check for the rest of the run, just acted like limpets and clung to a West London hasher.

Running Log

Event:	**The Tough Guy**
Distance:	**9 miles+**
Date:	**January 30th**

I had secured a place on the start list for the '94 Tough Guy. This was an event way ahead of its' time, dreamt up by the Tough Guy Guru, none other than Billy Wilson.

First staged in 1987 and organised by Billy Wilson under the pseudonym of 'Mr. Mouse', it is held on a 600-acre farm in the English village of Perton, Staffordshire. Before he began staging the Tough Guy, Billy Wilson was already known as a high-profile organiser of road running races and a sometimes eccentric participant. He most notably took part in the first London Marathon in 1981 dressed as a pantomime horse to raise funds for his Tettenhall Horse Sanctuary (which is the principal beneficiary of the Tough Guy event).

A former Grenadier Guard and trained soldier in the British Army, Wilson was among the pioneers of the running boom in Britain in the 1980s. He helped found the Wolverhampton Road Runners club, of which he became chairman. From 1982 to 1987 he organized the annual Wolverhampton Marathon. Increasing traffic, some drop in numbers (it was a traditionally a March Marathon), and legislation, saw Wilson shift his focus to his off-road events, staged on his own land, which have been extremely successful.

This year started off with a couple of Tough race events. It seemed that the multi-terrain running events had really taken off and a number of 'odd ball' events started to appear on the race calendar. First was the Tough Guy, then followed by the Nightmare 10. Early season mud-baths are the stuff of legend and build stamina for the warmer climes later in the year. I didn't run too much cross country in those early days. I relied on a good shiggy test with the hash on a Sunday morning. Always 5 or 6 miles with the reward of a pint at the pub.

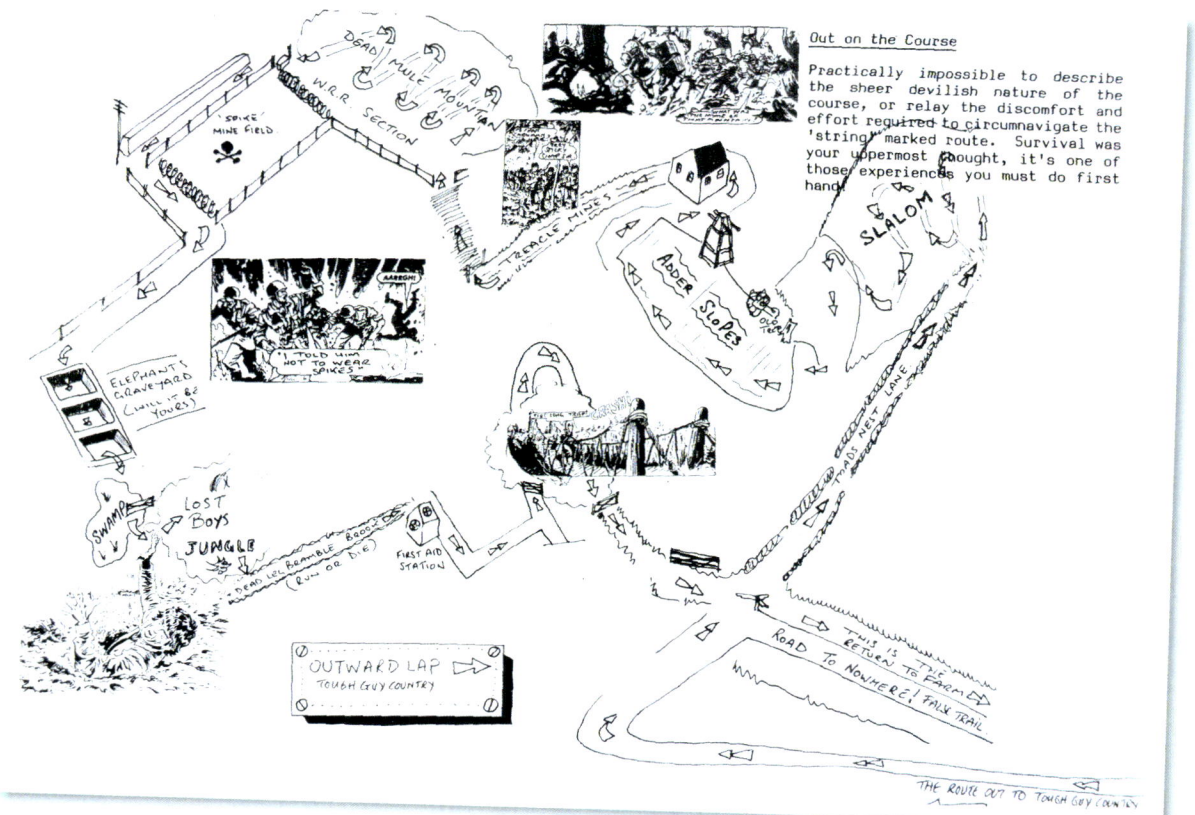

Out on the Course

Practically impossible to describe the sheer devilish nature of the course, or relay the discomfort and effort required to circumnavigate the 'string' marked route. Survival was your uppermost thought, it's one of those experiences you must do first hand.

including many 50-metre slalom runs up and down a steep hill, (the year I ran it there were 6), over 6 feet deep mud and water filled ditches (resembling the Battle of the Somme), log jumps, followed by an assault course. It claimed to be tougher than any other publicly accessible race worldwide, featuring over 25 obstacles through, under and over freezing water pools, rope bridges, nets and so on...

Up to the ankles in it...

However, late in January and still in the midst of winter came the TOUGH GUY with the Trained Soldier.

It's a famous - or should I say infamous - large scale event these days with corporate entries, designer finishing merchandise, even proper post-race facilities. Yes it's a big money event these days.

However, it wasn't always like that, the venue of course was the Tettenhall Horse Sanctuary, the Hoof Hospital, set in over 600 acres of farmland, and with a dedicated caring staff who take in and care for all sorts of horrific animal cruelty cases. But, for one day a year the barns and pens are transformed into a heaving mass of multicoloured runners. The day had dawned bright, but an icy wind lowered that chill factor. Most of the competitors were huddled up in the Donkey Barns, crouching behind bales of straw to keep out of the freezing wind. "Still its not as cold as a couple of years ago" piped up some Tough Guy Vet. 'The marshals had to break the ice on the lake', which by all accounts incurred 14 broken ankles and a dozen cases of hypothermia.

The Tough Guy race is staged over a course of over 9 miles or so. It is a total cross-country run,

With nigh-on 2,000 entries the demand was high and as a consequence the start was delayed by fifteen minutes. Eventually we made it out to the start area, strategically situated next to the silage bins, Nice! Because of the demand (numbers of runners on a narrow cross country course) runners had been seeded with different coloured bibs to indicate which group and pens they were in.

The elite in Lycra were up near the tape touching toes and stretching, getting primed for the air horn. The groups were to start in one minute intervals. Next in order were the 'Wet Necks' I was in the next group called the 'Wobble Muckers'.

My training had gone particularly to plan and I was keen to do well. I didn't really want to be stuck behind all and sundry, so I nonchalantly started to creep forward from the back of the WM's. No one paid much attention as everyone is; A) a bit nervous, and B) fucking freezing. I moved up the side of the holding pen and positioned myself at the front. It was then, just as I was congratulating myself, that I was spotted. What I had forgotten was that each different group had separate coloured bibs and being a Wobble Mucker at the front of the Wet Necks group I stood out a mile. Next thing I was grabbed unceremoniously by two burly fluorescent bibbed Marshalls and marched across the muddy start - in front of jeering runners and spectators - and thrown in jail! Well, it was an old wooden Horse Box. In any case I was locked in and made to wait until dead last. That's right, I was eventually let out after everybody had cleared the first hurdle, plus of course subject to generally good-natured abuse as I gave chase.

Lulled into a false sense of security the start is actually downhill. However, on this day a sharp hairpin soon followed with a drop into a flooded mud pit. The leaders were (I assume) able to leap for dry ground. However, the chasing horde fell in or were pushed in. Once out of this it was a Boys' Own cross country chase your Games Master would have been proud of. It was made up of around 6 or 7 miles which were interspersed with trail sections. In total around a nine mile course.

I made my way out to the country catching up a few people as I went. We came to a cross roads, it was Toads Nest lane. Here we were given baling twine with instructions from Marshals NOT to lose it. For fear of more reprisals I've never gripped a piece of string so tightly! At the end of **Toads Nest Lane** (a narrow muddy footpath), a slalom lay in wait. A series of 6 snaking hill climbs up through fern and bracken which reduced many to a walk as the legs turned to jelly. Next on to **Adder Slopes** and a nasty jog along an off-cambered path. Still, it gave you time to get a second wind, just in time to lose it in the **Treacle Mines**.

The Treacle Mines consisted of a rock-strewn track deliberately flooded with ankle-deep freezing water. It was a relief getting back out onto ploughed fields again. Next was **Dead Mule Mountain**, yet more hill climbs. Again some more cross country followed and by now you had found your race pace, a notch up from dead slow. Looking back across my shoulder I could see the impressive sight of hillsides woven with a zigzag of runners. It was a short fillip, but something I needed. So as I plod on behind the bloke in front I guess he's some sixty yards in front. Suddenly I look up and he's disappeared. As I approach the spot I can

see why - I have about a 9ft drop into a concrete tank. This is the **Elephants Graveyard**, and there were not one, but three of them.

These concrete bunkers took some agility to get in and out off. A couple of straw bales acted as landing base and steps, but when I hit them they had already started to break up into clumps. Thankfully on the last tomb the guy in front waited, as was now the custom to give me a helping hand out. I in turn waited for the runner behind me.

All this was still out in the midst of Tough Guy Country where all the obstacles are totally deliberate. Next I jogged on to **Lost Boys Jungle**, a swamp area where the only escape was along **Dead Leg Bramble Brook**. This was a grit-bottomed stream, which filled your trainers and used your socks as a sieve whilst trailing brambles ripped at your flesh. This lasted for around a 300yd stretch

before some more 'Jungle' and a warm wade through a swamp, chest high of course. Here I encountered a first aid post, the St Johns boys and girls being kept very busy. It was also the end of the first ordeal (lap).

I was now back to the cross roads and here the significance of the piece of string was revealed. Barring our way were a swat team of Marshall's collecting the baling string. No string meant you had to complete another lap! Jeez, I gleefully handed over my piece of baling twine and breathed a sigh of relief. So what now, a gentle trot back to the sanctuary and sanity? No, just the beginning of a second loop. It started gently enough across some old rabbit warrens and some scattered car tyres to stumble over and then an old rickety bridge. But then, wow – no more pussy footing - this was where the tough got going!

The inclusion of these trails would have graced any war film epic from Platoon to Bridge over the River Kwai. **Dead Leg Marsh** – a quick sand where, if you stood still for too long, you sunk without trace. Next the **Tunnel of Hell**, a belly crawl through a claustrophobic rat hole of a metal pipe, then onto the lake followed by the cargo nets climb. Are you keeping up?

Water, water everywhere – Not a drop to Drink. Water was now the obsession. If I was ever going to catch dysentery this was it. A plunge into a filthy stream then run up a hill, then back down the hill to the filthy stream and in again. Around a marker pole. Out of the stream, then run up the hill and then back down the hill into the filthy stream once more. Well, you get the idea, this we had to repeat several times, which I found very futile and irritating (was this the psychological test?). I eventually moved on from the ditch to some wooden ramps, followed by what looked like strawberry nets to be crawled under, elbows and knees fashion. However, it was barbed wire - my bum was now in shreds.

Eventually the battle was nearly over as I rounded the final stretch. However, placed on the run-in were those huge straw bales wrapped in plastic to climb over, and then finally the **Scorpions Tail** - an uphill finish. Aghhh! The agony is finally over, into a bin liner and shuffle over to get a polystyrene cup of hot sweet tea. The entry fee then was £23.00.

My advice: don't enter unless you're supremely fit or a masochist - or both!.

TIME: 2.15.55

Running Log

Event: **Weston-super-Mare, Tough Ten**
Distance: **10 miles**
Date: **February**

Running Log

Event: **Hereford 20**
Distance: **20 miles**
Date: **6th March**

Another foul morning cowering for cover on the beach front at Weston, but nevertheless, a huge field had assembled. Thankfully this race still exists (I seem to give so many the kiss of death). It's now in its third guise.

No frills or novelty for this event. This had certainly attracted the more committed runner, judging by the amount of club vests and emaciated occupants. Not a huge field for this race, so sticking to the game plan was essential (if only I could read the splits written on the back of my hand). Starting from the Hereford Leisure Centre, it was a quiet country lanes affair.

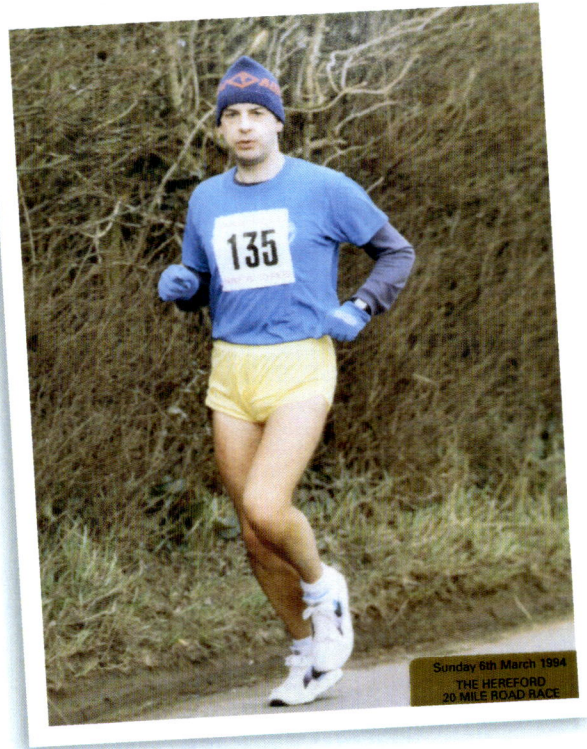

Originally the St Valentines Massacre 12, then the Tough Ten, it's now called the Two Bays Tough Ten. Leaving the gale off the sea front, I paced myself along the promenade and early street loops which made up around three miles, before heading off into the dunes then the woods. From what I could tell it tracked most of the original route, it still contained the testing trails within Worlebury Wood, and the semi moorland on the Sandy Bay headland.

The finish - of course - was on the famous sands, so after the respite of tarmac for a mile or so, the course dropped down onto the beach, just to sap those legs a bit more. And while we were out running some wise guy had built a huge sand hill with the help of a JCB. This we had to first clamber over before we could see the finishing line.

TIME: 1.11.43

Not a lot of support out on course either, which consisted of one small loop followed by the large loop. I finished comfortable just a minute outside my target time.

TIME: 2.31.06

My winter training regime continued as I programmed in a couple of local events to build in some base work, endurance for the up coming London (Marathon) in April. First down to the West Country to Weston-Super-Mare without a bucket and spade and then onto the wilds of Herefordshire. Finally I entered again the endurance tester down in deepest Wales, another twenty miles to top up the mileage around the beautiful lakes.

It was all going so, so well, and with London just a few weeks away, my mileage taper began. Then on my return to work after a lunchtime run, my calf tweaked and I tore a muscle. It was pretty sore and even with two or three visits to the physiotherapist table along with ultrasound, it couldn't put Humpty together again. To soften the blow (which it didn't) I could carry my guaranteed place over to the following year's race.

I was gutted, but over that winter I probably put together my best marathon training (ever) with good weekly totals, not David Bedford mileage agreed, but on par with the other guys at Tewkesbury AC. It took time to get back to running after that blow, plus the calf niggle persisted. Went back to the Hash of course, and finally got back to racing in late summer with two of my fondest events.

LONDON
94
Withdrawn

Running Log

Event:	**Race the Train**
Distance:	**14 Miles**
Date:	**August**

Yes, as daft as it seems. The idea is to beat the narrow gauge train up a Welsh mountainside. Again, this was something that appealed to me as something different. Besides, it was a quirky race distance when every event seems to be a 10K race. Tywyn is in Mid Wales, a seaside resort on the Cardigan Bay coast, and it's a bit of a trek to get there from England, so many of the runners make a weekend of it, and it has become quite a festival. It's a Saturday afternoon event which adds to the flavour, as the small town is swamped for the weekend.

Running for the train

Come race day, the train sits steaming away in the station with excited family and friends climbing on board to get a close-up view of the race from the carriages. Its hard not to get tense as we line up with all the hullabaloo. The small town centre start is packed as the race begins.

As with many a fell race, it starts gentle enough in green pasture, before Welsh farm tracks become steep and the order of the day. The route of course follows right beside the train track. The sense and anxiety of being 'chased' by the train is quite unreal and adds to your pace, which until you get caught is at an unsustainable rate. It was first ran apparently in 1984, the brainchild of a local dentist (if you didn't think dentists were sadistic here's your proof!).

The full race is 14 miles or thereabouts, as the route can alter slightly, and is an out and back chase.

You cross the track at Brynglais Station and head on to Abergynolwyn, the halfway mark. I made the turn in 53 minutes. The course is mostly over public footpaths and local privately-owned farmland, with the permission of the landowners and is scenic to the extreme. You pass Dolgoch on your return and 'run in' on the outward trail. I enjoyed my race AFTER I was overtaken by the train, which chugged past me at the ten mile mark, I could relax and take in the race and scenery. Only the elite runners stay ahead of the train for the full distance. The train does stop in various locations to take on water and pass other trains, so it is an achievable challenge - for some!

The Rotary Club organise each event with growing success, and the 2024 race will be the 39th event. The 2008 race saw a start entry of 822 with a course record set at 1hr 18min.

TIME: 1.55.09

Full steam ahead

14th ANNUAL
RACE THE TRAIN
TYWYN MID-WALES
SATURDAY 16th AUGUST 1997
ONE OF THE 1997
SAUCONY RACE SERIES
14 MILE 384 YDS SENIOR RACE
5 MILE JUNIOR RACES
5 MILE FUN RUN
10 KILOMETRE RACE

CLOSING DATE
2nd August

FULL DETAILS & ENTRY FORM (SAE)
ROTARY CLUB OF TYWYN,
C/O 7 YR YNYS,
FAENOL ISAF,
TYWYN, GWYNEDD LL36 0DW
TEL: 01654 710667
(OFFICE HOURS)

Never guess who I had in the back of me cab

This is a tale which takes our reader to the backwaters of Shepherd's Bush one winters evening in the mid 1990s. I was a frequent visitor to various hashes across the UK back then, and West London was a particular favourite. I had it off pat, an early skive off work, pick up a couple of willing cohorts and we were off; A40, M40, then ditch the car in Hillington Tube. This was where the neon lights started to flash down to the ticket booth. Remember, this was some 30 years ago where ticket halls and British Rail staff were present to purchase tickets from. You may recall that said people were not always of the most cheerful disposition. We all bought return tickets then asked what time the last train back was. Whatever time he mumbled it wasn't late enough for a few beers and a curry, so we all changed our tickets for singles. Can you imagine how delighted he was to do this for us?

Down the stairs to the platform to a waiting train, all hopped on board. A few minutes passed and nothing. Change of driver we reassured ourselves, then the lights go out. On jumps a BR cockney sparrow "sorry lads, train's in for service". Brilliant! So hopes of making the run now were disappearing fast as an agonising quarter of an hour passed before a new train arrived. Eventually we rumbled into Marylebone and sought out the pub. The designated pub - Gloucester Arms (closed in 2005) was difficult to spot in the dark, unrecognisable being behind scaffolding and plaster boarding. We dumped our bags where one of our party (Bilko) decided to stay put as he felt at home in a builders yard.

So the rest of us set off after the West London pack, and by sheer athleticism and short cutting caught them up – perhaps things are looking up? A decent hash run followed by a few beers back in the GA. All too soon it was time to leave and perhaps take in a curry house before heading back to Gloucestershire. We agreed on heading back and on route would pop up at a tube station a bit nearer our car and a cheaper option. We settled on Shepherd's Bush.

We expected to see a tasty tandoori from the entrance steps to the tube – we didn't. Remember this is long before the miracle of mobile phone apps and handheld computers, we just had to lick and hold a wet finger in the air or sniff on the breeze for the nose to detect a balti treat. We chose a direction and wandered off for what seemed ages to find a restaurant, anyway we found one, and piled in and ordered the necessary and started on the lime pickle and popadoms. Towards the end of meal any faint hope of catching a tube had evaporated, and we had well and truly missed the last train. Still no worries, we'll call a cab – well, the owner of the restaurant did. This wasn't uncommon back then and Uber wasn't a thing.

So, bill paid, we all fall out of the Curry House into a bundle on the pavement, where the cold night air meets the warm glow of a Madras head on – Belch. Ooops. Pardon.

Right where's this taxi ? We scanned the high street of Shepherd's Bush, nothing. I expected to see one of those shiny black jobs which whizz around Hyde park Corner, but no such luck. Not a for hire to be seen anywhere. Suddenly a car door opened onto the pavement. I peered into the black shadowy interior where the occupant growled in a Deli accent – you taxi ?

Well, as the sober one of the party, clearly the situation was a little dodgy. However, my drunken compadres didn't hesitate and were in the back of the cab in no time, and at 1.30 in the morning I didn't have much of an argument. So stepping into an unmarked unregistered car (cab) with one heavyweight ethnic minority in a dingy back street was the only option. Besides there were four of us (admittedly pissed), and only one of him – besides I didn't fancy walking – so I'm in the front. After 10 minutes and the third visit to the same set of traffic lights. I begin to get suspicious, we appeared to be going round in circles. Was this an attempt to raise the fare, if so as I was sober, I rumbled him. After several exchanges of "You do know where Hillington Station is?" with the return of a grunt and very little else. Next our man stops the car and gets out and - wait for it - phones the Curry House for directions!! The titters and giggles from our trio of hash chums in the back turn to hails of tear-streaming laughter as I suggest we 'make a run for it – bail out while we could'. Too late, he was back and off we went again. I wasn't the least bit confident that he would find the station, and sure enough we stop again, this time to ask at a petrol station. The clueless driver returned completely facial expressionless however mine was doing contortions – I'd had enough. Time to co-pilot me thinks. "Oh, I recognise this bit, its left at the top", he could just about understand my terse English and I didn't really have a clue I was praying we'd see a road sign. It was the blind leading the dumb. But as luck would have it within a few minutes we were approaching Hillington Station car park.

For me it was relief. For the boys in the back it meant they at least had stopped laughing and cracking jokes. I expected at least a mumbled apology and perhaps a reduced fee – instead he wanted £20 (that's £40 in today's money). I went into orbit – "You must be Ffffing Joking! We've been all round London you didn't even know the way - you've had to ask twice!" Rant Rant. My passing shot was "£40 quid? I wouldn't pay that for Fred Housego. Bye." Now I'm out of the car throwing my arms around and making off towards my car. I think he did get paid by one of the Three Cavaliers, more for entertainment value than a competent taxi service. I don't think I've ever been back to West London hash since, and certainly not in a taxi.

Moral of Tale: Tube ticket in hand is worth more than a curry in Shepherds Bush.

Open: 12noon–2.30p.m. & 6.00p.m.–11.45p.m.

AJANTA TANDOORI
Fully Licensed & Air Conditioned

10–12 Goldhawk Road,
Shepherds Bush,
London W12.
Telephone: (081) 743 5191

Buffet Parties Catered for:
Take Away Service Available

Running Log

Event: **Polytechnic 1994**
Distance: **26.2 miles**
Date: **September**

Out of all my running exploits, this event is easily my favourite and my most treasured medal and memory. As with many of my racing tales, it's another classic race that has succumbed to commercial pressures. The rising entry fees and the inability these days to close roads, due to the pressure on the public purse, has seen many traditional club events disappear.

It initially lost ground (of course) to the more glamorous upstart the London Marathon. The popularity of the race was already in decline by the time I got to run it the Autumn of 1994. The Poly as it was fondly called, was literally the stuff of legends. It really is a classic race to mourn, and is still held in tremendous affection by runners who have graced the course, and by those who wish they had.

Here I digress into its' back story which really puts the event and history into context. I think it's worth going into detail here as names like Jim Peters and Dorando Pietri are synonymous with this course and race.

The Polytechnic Marathon had its origins in the marathon of the 1908 Summer Olympics, held in London. Following the 1904 Summer Olympics held in the USA, the IOC gave the task of organising to the British Olympics Association which had to include the 'new' race. However, the marathon was a sticking point, they had no experience of organising a race of that length. The distance would vary from race to race, it just had to be over 25 miles (40K). There was some vague attempt at plotting out a course, but it wasn't until late on in 1907 that the On Sec of the Polytechnic Harriers (Jack Andrew) offered to take on the task, the BOA readily agreed. In modern speak 'snapped his hand off'.

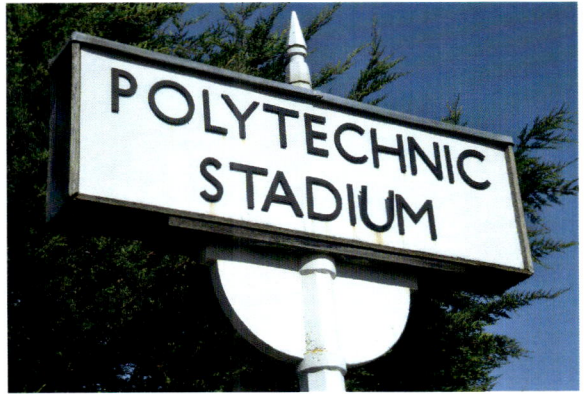

The Polytechnic Harriers were 'the' athletics club of the era with the University actually in Regent Street. They settled on the notion of starting the race at Windsor Castle and winding its way through the west boroughs to the Olympic Stadium at White City. A trial run was held in the April of 1908 where the course ran short and finished near Wembley. When the White City was finally constructed an idea was put forward of constructing a tunnel beneath the royal box. However, this had to be scrapped as the finish entry for the runners as it was reserved for carriages. Therefore another entry was decided upon with the finish line in front of the Royal Box. The entry point meant a near lap of the track to the finish line, a distance that turned out to be the fabled 26 miles, 385 yards.

The 1908 Summer Games Marathon was very much a novelty, but drew a lot of pubic attention. The actual race and finish itself was clouded in controversy due to the disqualification of the actual winner, Italian Baker, Dorando Pietri. Pietri chose a slow pace over the first half of the course, slowly overtaking the field and catching the leader at Wormwood Scrubs. Here he sped up and reached the stadium with a good lead. However, he was in trouble as fatigue and dehydration had taken its toll. He entered the stadium, but started the lap in the wrong direction. Officials ran to guide him to the correct way but he fell. It took him a further four falls and ten minutes before he crossed the finish line, once more stumbling into the arms of an official. The Americans, as their man had finished second were quick to lodge the protest of receiving outside assistance, and was awarded the Gold Medal.

Johnny Hayes   USA   2.55.18
William Clarke   GB   3.16.08

The dramatic conclusion to the finish of the 1908 Olympic race really grabbed the public's attention. The collapse of the 'little guy' appealing to the British sense of championing the underdog. However, there was also considerable disappointment among the public, that the British runners had fared poorly. The Sporting Life Newspaper, sensing this public interest, and in an attempt to improve matters, put up a magnificent trophy for an annual international marathon that would become second only in importance to the Olympic event itself.

The Polytechnic Harriers were again asked to organise the event, and the Polytechnic Marathon was born.

1908 Summer Games Marathon Winner Dorando Pietri

Poly Notables
Among such men who won the 'Poly' in the 1960s, when Callard & Bowser sponsored the race, included Ron Hill (Bolton United Harriers), who went on to reach the pinnacle of marathon success by winning the European, Commonwealth and Boston titles and then returned to the 'Poly' at the age of 39 in 1977 to finish second in a time (2hr.16m.37s) which,in most other years,would have been good enough to win. He was unfortunate that day to come up against Ian Thompson.

'Buddy' Edelen, of America & Hadleigh Olympiads, who came to this country in 1960 after the disappointment of failing to make the U.S. Olympic team, and set the fastest recorded time in the world in 1963 with 2hr.14m.26s, on the old Windsor-Chiswick course.

Basil Heatley (Coventry Godiva), who warmed up for his Olympic silver medal in 1964 by winning the Poly in another worlds best of 2hr.13m.55s.

Morio Shigematsu (Japan), the winner in 1965, who broke Heatley's record with a time of 2hr.12m.00s.

The build up my Poly
Not a common occurrence, but it's another race with a start at A and finish at B, with a 'gap' of 26 miles of thought-out logistics required. I had decided to overnight in Windsor itself, as travel on the morning of a race is always fractious. Therefore, I needed to stow my car (works van) near the finish area and thus I wouldn't have to stagger far with my kit bag and wobbly legs. I located the sports stadium and finish and carefully parked up in a leafy suburban side street just a few minutes' walk away. Hopefully all this effort and planning would pay off when it came to the race itself as I felt I was in good nick for a good time if things went to plan. The train journey from Chiswick to Eton and Windsor took about an hour.

Now back in Windsor it was around tea time. It was a pleasant warm evening and as I was travelling light I was able to wander using my sketch map to locate the youth hostel. This was in a very nice quaint area of the town. I was a member of the Youth Hostel Association, so check-in was painless. Now to bag a bed in one of the dormitories, as this was now down time (I should be resting my legs) and up on my bunk to devour the race instructions and course details for the umpteenth time. Apart from getting your legs up 24hrs before the race, another tip from Brendan Foster was have a beer the night before. He always had a Guinness pre-race to quell any race butterflies and help him sleep.

This was one piece of advice I wasn't going to ignore. According to my trusty Good Beer Guide, Windsor had several Real Ale pubs worth checking out. Not being a huge fan of the black stuff I avoided that, but did down a few pints in two or three excellent pubs (most particularly the Swan in Clewer Village). By the time I'd staggered back to the youth hostel I hadn't a shred of nerves. It was still fairly early - around ten o'clock - and with the disturbance of to-ing and fro-ing of the dorm, I didn't get to sleep soundly. I was now rueing the choice of accommodation - perhaps my budget approach wasn't the best idea. I did get some sleep, but not nearly enough. The slumber I did manage was shattered further at around 3.30am Sunday morning as the fire alarm went off. The drill practice was to leave all possessions and file out

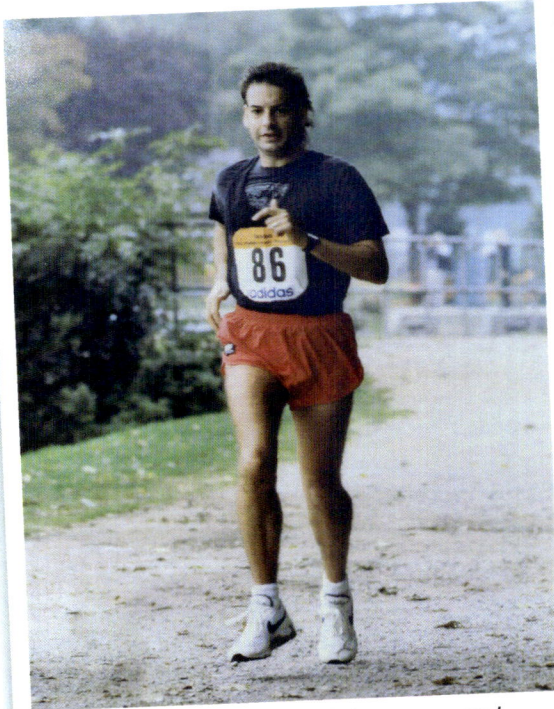

No time to stop and smell the roses, as I complete the Kew Gardens loop.

through the corridor and out into the tiny side street. It appeared to be a false alarm, but the Fire Brigade were on their way, we could hear the sirens as they approached. They duly arrived and while the men investigated the building, we shivered in the damp air and cold temperature. This preparation was definitely not in the Brendan Foster 'how to run a marathon' guide.   I'm on the start line in less than five hours' time and here I am on the pavement in my PJs. With cool drizzle to accompany my return and the other hostlers back to bed I salvaged what kip I could.

The Race

For the 1994 race the Polytechnic Marathon start was at Windsor Home Park, site of the Royal Windsor Horse

Show. A glorious warm morning it was too. Most of the runners had sought what shade they could before being assembled. With the 'thrill' of an A-B course it added another level of excitement. Trying to contain myself, I was in good nick for a decent run and the sleepless night wasn't playing on my mind too much at this stage.

The early stages were at a keen pace as we headed toward and on and through the picturesque Datchet village, then dipping under the M25 towards Staines. After the 6-mile water and sponge station, we turned right into Church Street. This slope drops you down to the river and the first section of Thames riverside (by-passing Staines town centre).

On through Laleham village, after which Shepperton film studios were to your left. I was in need of the third water station just before Shepperton (10 miles). I had now relaxed into my run and was enjoying the course. Hampton Court Palace was soon reached, the famous maze to the right, not a time to veer off course! Back over the river at Kingston with a modern twist after all the historical sights, we pass under the tunnel with the John Lewis department store above.

With some irony here the course then went down River Lane, past the front gate of the former London Marathon supremo himself, Chris Brasher, at the 20 mile point. Here we join the tow-path which has a few obstacles, namely tourists and cobbles by the boat houses. The lapping of the mighty Thames ends at Richmond Lock as the course now headed away from the river and across the Old Deer Park (22 miles). The wonderful laid out Kew Gardens gave one a lift as no question I was feeling pretty knackered by now. How I was rueing my broken nights sleep. A monstrosity hove into view next; the concrete bunker of the Public Records Office.

I just had to get over Chiswick Bridge and ignore the Fuller's Brewery, I sure could do with a pint! The famous University Boat finish was to the right, but I needed to get to the other side of the bridge first. After crossing I needed Hartington Road, and here it was and the Polytechnic Stadium (University of Westminster Stadium). This was a fantastic feeling, not quite White City, but certainly the nearest footsteps I could follow in this wonderful old race. I completed the three-quarters of a lap of the track before finishing in front of the grandstand.

I think myself lucky as the demise came in 1996, just two years later. The Poly was Europe's oldest regular marathon, it had seen more world records and its course had been run over more often than any other marathon. So to run the original A-B course (near as dammit) was a great privilege.

By the 1970s the Polytechnic Harriers and the Poly Marathon were in decline. Traffic problems made it difficult to continue with the Windsor to Chiswick route, and from 1973 until 1992 the race was restricted to loops of the Windsor area. Performances declined, and so did the status of the Poly Marathon. With the introduction of mass marathons and the London Marathon on its door step, and big-money events elsewhere, the Poly Marathon could not compete.

Another happy coincidence was the Team Award victors as below:

3	Steve Robinson	Cheltenham Harriers AAC	
16	Paul Kinsella	Cheltenham Harriers AAC	
18	Richard Rogan	Cheltenham Harriers AAC	
37			
1	Christopher Buckley	Westbury Harriers	2 21 57
205	**Graham Robinson**	**Tewkesbury AC**	**3 29 36**

Token Trophy

My story doesn't quite end there. As I briefly described as an incentive and marketing tool the newspaper 'Sporting Life' presented a handsome trophy to the organisers to awarded to the winners Polytechnic Harriers duly put their new acquisition on display at their Regent Street headquarters until security became a concern. From there it was stored in the Victoria and Albert Museum. By the 1970s the Polytechnic Harriers and the Poly Marathon were, as previously described, sadly in decline. There was a brief resurrection of the event In the 1980s, when the London Road Runners Club took up organizing the Poly Marathon under licence.

The said trophy was loaned to them for display at the finish of the race. Eventually however the LRRC folded and the magnificent trophy ended up stored in someone's basement. Here it languished forgotten and gathering dust. That is until a reader's letter to the Daily Mirror in 1990 enquired 'what had happened to the distinguished trophy?'. In the intervening years the Mirror Group had bought up the Sport Life newspaper and had no clue as to 'what trophy'? They certainly had no idea of its' whereabouts, citing 'it must have been lost in the war', not understanding that it had actually been presented to race winners up to 1961.

Anything seem familiar? The first recipients of the 'new trophy' Radcliffe & Abera - 2003 Marathon Winners

Subsequently a letter was then sent to the Mirror saying 'we've got it and the trophy is in safe keeping. The correspondence was from the then secretary David Barrington of Kingston AC and Polytechnic Harriers. This galvanised the newspaper giant into action and they reclaimed the trophy and assumed responsibility for its keeping. For the next few Poly races the Grand Trophy was displayed at the finish. However, this all ended the very year I did my race.

The 1984 Polytechnic Marathon race director Ian Ridpath's attention was piqued by a London Marathon Press Release. 'The trophy, owned by Mirror Group Newspapers is on permanent loan to the event, and that the Sporting Life Trophy would henceforth be presented jointly to the men's and women's London Marathon champions'.

Ian's protests and historical reference of the famous old trophy simply fell on deaf ears. The Mirror Group wouldn't acknowledge that the Polytechnic Harriers had a rightful claim to the trophy. After Brasher's death in February 2003, the glorious and now controversial piece of silverware, was also renamed the Chris Brasher Sporting Life Trophy.

Being a proud member the Hash House Harrier movement I've attended some memorable Hash Events at both National and on the International stage. Some have produced some memorable hash trails and running experiences and others some memorable drinking bouts! If you've not stumbled across a hash pack in full cry, you're missing out on some very varied running and oh so important, sociability.

HASHING
The ethos of Hashing is very simple :-
- *To promote physical fitness among our members*
- *To get rid of weekend hangovers*
- *To acquire a good thirst and to satisfy it in beer*
- *To persuade older members that they are not as old as they feel.*

My thanks to Ian Ridpath, writer, editor, encyclopedist and broadcaster, for the in-depth background to the Poly.

So apart from my athletic pursuits, I thought it only fair to include some wild Hash weekends which gave me most pleasure. Here is one such event.

Euro Hash

Euro Hash was coined for the inaugural event staged by the Paris H3. A European Hash hosting a weekend of running and partying in the most sensual of cities. The event proved a success and has subsequently being organised every couple of years (or thereabouts), Prague being the host in 2021 and Eurohash 2025 will be in Tallinn, Estonia, 14th – 17th of August 2025.

Euro Hash – the story so far…

An impetuous move in 1992 saw the superb mismanagement talents of Paris H3 declare 'Euro Hash' – an Intercontinental extravaganza (although several European hash's were disgruntled at this initiative initially). The Paris Euro Hash did attract some 1000 hasher's and not just from Europe. Champagne parties under the Eiffel tower and a jog around the cities historic city sights set the seal on a marvellous weekend. The pièce de résistance being the On On in the Cirque d'hivier with the sight of the Paris Harriet's doing the Can Can. Now follow that…

Well, down to Spain for 1993, and our hosts the Madrid Hash. Mountainous runs left scars on many hashers' souls, whilst REAL Bull fighting left scars on hashers' bodies. For the 1994 event, the occasion hit a snag as no one fancied taking on the mantel. It was an onerous task. Eventually a last minute event took place in Germany and incredibly, for the 4th event, Euro Hash was held in a War Zone. As Zagreb came forward and hosted the event on the Island of Jelsa (Croatia) not surprisingly numbers were down!

However, my only Euro Hash and my stand-out momentous event happened in Brussels.

Belgium is the capital of Europe, and some would say brewing, so Brussels seemed the perfect fit.

Running Log

Event: **Euro Hash Summer In The City**
Distance: **Varied**
Date: **July 25th - 27th 1997 VUB**

The party site was housed at a university campus about 12k from the city centre where most of the participants (hashers) were, naturally, holed up in hotels. The to-ing and fro-ing did become tedious, even with the frequent Metro trains. The late night shuttle bus was the saviour as the Metro shut down at midnight. The campus had erected a candy striped orange and white marquee, and a few side booths were scattered around and about for promo merchandise and snacks.

Only a small walk away was the University's enormous refectory where on Friday a sumptuous meal was served. In the aforementioned Marquee itself was an impressive bar, set up either side of the arena with three top notch Belgium beers and (in strict compliance of EEC guidelines), a glass washer.

Saturday - A choice of five different trails were available and held in the afternoon. I took the Waterloo run whose route took in historic battle sights. It was a long run, about 20K and around two hours, with a beer stop about halfway. More refreshment (beers) at the finish with customary hash circle. In the evening it was back up to the University for Dinner and the main party evening.

'No Brussels for me.'

Sunday - Thank Heaven

Wasn't it Maurice Chevalier who sang 'Thank Heaven for little girls'? Perhaps the hash congregation who witnessed the miracle played out on a cobbled corner of Rue de l'Etuve in olde Bruxelles should change the chorus to 'thank heaven for little boys'. It was as close to a virgin birth!

The early morning start (well, 10 o'clock) didn't look good for a gathering in downtown Brussels where the Hares hadn't shown up for the start of this (point) A – B run.

Finally the Hares arrived and described the course and its marking of green flour. So now was a whistle stop tour of the citys' best bits, starting with the Red Light district. The Guildhall and the Grand Place had close inspections, before diving down into narrow walkways and the old part of the City. On past a glut of pavement seafood restaurants to arrive and congregate at the shrine of the Manneken Pis.

The ornate stature on this occasion was bedecked in running attire and looking every bit like a Manneken Pis hasher. Some bottles of beer were handed out amongst the growing assembly of runners, while we waited for the miracle to happen.

VUB VRIJE UNIVERSITEIT BRUSSEL

Now, bearing in mind we had two Gendarmes looking on, the Mayor and a Belgium TV crew what odds would you give for turning water into BEER! Wait a minute, what's this? Amongst all the runners appeared a little chap in overalls rolling a beer keg along the pavement with a spaghetti of tubing under his arm. I was curious and followed him round the rear of the statue. Well, I couldn't believe it. I was like a little boy, nose pressed against the wrought iron railings as Monsieur Juplier got to work. Then the moment of truth. The audience lurched forward, somewhat reminiscent of the Kop at Anfield. The water continued to flow from the staute's appendage… then nothing… bated breath, and then a huge cheer as the beer came flowing and frothing out. It certainly was a privilege to have been on that run, and I guess to have seen my most memorable (to date) hash sight. Seeing beer fountain out of a National Monument - Brilliant.

Why is there a statue of a peeing boy in Brussels?
The statue's name, quite literally, means 'peeing little man', or 'peeing boy'. Before this became his title, he was also known as Petit Julien, or 'Little Julien'. There are many fables that surround his origins; some are believable, while others are downright bizarre. The most probable explanation has to do with the fact that there were many tanners on the Rue de l'tuve during the Middle Ages. It was not uncommon to let children urinate on leather since the ammonia in urine helps to make the leather more supple. Of course, there is no way of knowing whether Manneken Pis was truly an homage to the tanners. Another popular story states how the boy saved the city of Brussels. The legend goes that Brussels was surrounded by enemies who pretended to retreat, but in reality were hiding gunpowder underneath. A little boy named Julien saw the burning fuse and quickly peed on it. Out of gratitude, the city made a statue in his likeness.

Hashing - Bristol Fashion

Back in the mists of time, or to narrow it down to the last century, around 1984, another hashing incident is perhaps worth recalling. A weekend had been arranged to celebrate Bristols H3 (South West hash group) 100th run. For this milestone occasion a camp over was arranged on the outskirts of Wotton under Edge at a place called the Bull Pen. Formally a (you guessed it) a yard and shelter for a bull. The area was converted into a bar with a rudimentary campsite attached. The usual frivolity was in full flow from around lunchtime as hashers arrived and began to erect tents and frequent the bar.

The run started well enough, with not a full pack as many had decided to wait in the bar, but enough keen types were about to run the 100th hash run. After half an hour or so, after skirting North Nibley and the shadow of Tyndale's monument, we lost the trail. About four or five of us were scratching our heads and after a few minutes had passed by and a fruitless search for markings, came that eureka moment. "I bet its a drink stop at WB". WB is short for Waterly Bottom, an isolated hamlet one mile to the east of North Nibley. The New Inn is set in a remote valley with beautiful views of the surrounding hills.

So off we set, galloping toward the spot we knew so well, as it was a familiar Bristol Hash haunt with many runs being set from here. We arrived at the pub, the New Inn, not a sign of a marking not a sign of a hasher. Bit odd we thought. We milled around for a while, tried the door which was locked (2pm closing time those days).

Ruby Sainty, the Landlady, must be in, so after some shouting the occasional stone up at the upstairs window, Ruby appeared through the bathroom window, soap bubbles rolling off her shoulders and a bath towel around her head. "What's the noise, and what do you lot want?" She recognised a number in our group.

Hasher no.1:   We're waiting for the runners to come here for a beer stop

Ruby: *What Beer Stop?*

Hasher no. 2:   To mark our 100th run we thought we were having a beer stop here.

Ruby: *No. No one has arranged anything with me.*

All us hashers: SHIT!

Ruby: *Hang on – I'll come down and open up.*

And so she did bless her. Wrapped in a bath robe she let us enter the hallowed bar while we mused at what to do next. Having a beer seemed to be the consensus of opinion. Luckily the GM of the Bristol hash was in our company so beers were readily pulled while we waited – or so we thought. We finished our first pints and no sign of the Hash arriving at the New Inn. Hmmmm.

So a slate was secured in the Bristols GM name (good old Rob Newton) and we settled in (for the afternoon as it turned out). We also arranged for a taxi to take us all back to the camp site, as none of us were in a fit state to walk, let alone run back!

We poured into the taxi and in what seemed no time, us 'strays' were back at the camp site. No one had even realised we were missing. We weren't exactly 'ship shape' (hic), but it was Bristol Fashion.

Paradise Lost? (in a haze)

These days exotic races all over the globe entice runners and athletes to far flung places. You can race around the pyramids, jog past Eyres Rock and even test yourself up Mount Everest. I've been pretty fortunate to have run in some beautiful and memorable places, some of which I've covered in my Escapades. However, sometimes you just don't appreciate your surroundings, take in the views, as perhaps you should. I mean who wouldn't enjoy the beautiful and dramatic back-drop of Scottish Lochs and Hills, the scent of majestic pine forests? It was what we all see in the brochures and wonderful tourist board promotion.

Such an occasion occurred (sort of) back in 1995 as I travelled north for the Glasgow Hash 500th run. My route into the former City of Culture was greeted by huge bright yellow banners proclaiming 'Glasgow - Miles Better'. This lavish adornment complete with Mister Man logo was trying to cover up a shabby looking gasometer. With only a fleeting glimpse of the City's fine architecture from the M8, I climbed out of the urban sprawl on towards Drymen to find the weekends venue, Auchengilan Camp.

A wee dram

After settling into camp - registering and finding your wooden cabin - and if early enough bagging the best bunks! It was a wander down to the nearest hot spot. Make that the ONLY hotspot. Yes, we're talking remote, but the Carbeth Inn had a warm welcome. The hash have used this pub before and they were well used to the Hash and amicably tolerated the robust atmosphere and banner adornment across a balcony. A folk duo had feet thumping and heads nodding, whereas several pints of 80/ and three or four trays of sandwiches were devoured before the midnight curfew. The moonless sky made for a stumble and grope in the dark back to camp, where we found 'Dillys' - the Edinburgh Hash band - were in action. I managed to gyrate my hips a couple

of times I seem to remember, but at no one in particular. The next thing I remember was my bunk bed spinning endlessly – Thank god I had chosen the bottom bunk. Good night cruel world

Saturday

Breakfast was announced and it didn't seem like a good idea, in fact, very unappealing. Rigor mortis had set in. I couldn't move. Hashers returned from breakfast in readiness for the run. "Not up to Breakfast Robo? - lovely square sausage". The next thing - the last shout of 'the busses are leaving'. You not doing the run Robo? I had managed to put on some running gear and my trainers on the right feet. Stuffed my change of gear in a plastic bag and ventured outside. Perhaps some fresh sanitised Stirlingshire air may do the trick – it didn't.

Two coaches had been lined up ready to leave at 10.30 for the Glasgow 500th. I put off boarding the coach until the last possible moment, the last thing I needed was a hot stuffy bus ride. Unfortunately what I didn't figure on was leaving it last minute I didn't get a seat. So I sat cross legged in the aisle, missing all the scenic snow-capped mountain ranges against a clear blue sky. It was only 10 mins or so into the journey as the coach warmed up, began a swaying motion and I started to feel sick. Beads of sweat appeared on my brow. I wasn't - was I – God, I was gonna throw up - but where!?

Only place for it, I emptied out the change of clothes I'd packed in my carrier bag and promptly threw up in there. God what a sight. Oh God, what could be worst? Nothing you'd think. Well, think again. Glasgow Hash had thoughtfully laid on a boat trip across Loch Lomond.

The captain took one look at me and didn't want me across his gang plank. I looked so rough and pale he thought I had scurvy. Anyway, after some discussion Jim Akinhead convinced him I always look that and was fit for sea. He handed out the oranges and I went below deck.

Running Log

Event:	**GLASGOW 500th Trail**
Distance:	**9 miles**
Date:	**28th - 30th April 1995**

Two trails were on offer, starting with a boat cruise first (the one I was on) or the run first.
White trail – Rowardennan Lodge to Balmaha
Blue Trail – Balmaha to Rowardennan Lodge – clever eh? This was my trail.

Meanwhile, as the boat chugged across the Loch, I spent 40 minutes mostly hanging over the side. Despite my lack of sea legs the trip did show some beautiful scenery which the hardy hashers did appreciate. The run however was a different story.

The route was well marked in flour, but away from the quayside the trail went straight up Ben Lomond - all 974 metres of it! We made base camp at the first sign of snow flurries and waited for Sherpas. Mercifully, before we experienced oxygen depravation, the trail used a little-known goat run which roller-coastered around the side of the munros, the loch glistering below in the distance. So far I hadn't ran a step, walking was my limit, but then not many hashers had either.

After all that climbing over the next hour we steadily lost altitude and returned to the shores, of making our way through campsites at Cashel and Milarrochy. Wafts of smoking barbecues made me hungry, and by now I had shaken off my hangover. At last we arrived at Balmaha, the lead runners making it back in a little over two hours. For us mere mortals (with generous amounts of short cutting and an ice cream stop), we strolled in at two hours 30mins, or three hours depending on the queue at Mr whippy.

Glasgow Miles Wetter
The next day I managed breakfast with as many boiled eggs as you could carry (cock up on the catering front), and last nights supper leftovers of onion bhajis. It was a misty start and very wet footing - torrential rain overnight meant shiggy underfoot. It was also a much better hash run. The trail took in pine woods and Scottish peat bogs which, judging by the colour of my socks, undisturbed for centuries. We again ran along the West Highland way where it led to a regal regroup at Mugdock Castle. The On Home was across some golf links and three quarters of a mile killer uphill finish.

However, I saw the scenic highlands (alcoholic haze or not), and it was certainly a treasure trove of a memory, and never more has the famous song by Will Fyffe been more appropriate:

"But when I get a couple of drinks on a Saturday, Glasgow belongs to me"

Loch Lomond

Running Log

Event:	**Nutra Sweet London Marathon**
Distance:	**26.2 miles**
Date:	**2nd April 1995**

So back to London and bitter sweet one for me (and not just the saccharin taste of the main sponsor). This was the 15th staging of the race and the third and final year of Nutra Sweet involvement. I'd picked up my number from the Olympia Exhibition hall on the Thursday using it as a dummy run, as I was planning on parking out of town and using the tube early on race day morning.

I caught the district line from Ealing Broadway and then via the marathon trains out of Charing Cross. I made it to the start line bright and early I wasn't taking any chances with the trains this year. Whilst I kicked about on Greenwich some four years on, I noticed a whole lot more people, several thousand I'd say, which made moving around more difficult and visiting a loo a tough life decision. Do I stand in a queue for twenty minutes in the wind or just relax and keep warm next to the baggage lorries.

The wait, which was interminable, was eventually ended by the cannon and finally the race started. But of course we didn't move. It took me over eight minutes to reach the starting gantry. Remember this was back when there was no such thing as a timing chip, so you had to use your own time and ignore any timings on the course, otherwise you'd speed up and increase your chances of hitting the wall.

The plan was to run at an 8 min mile pace, and I'd placed myself in the 3.45 – 4.00 just to be on the safe side and get me off to a slower, but steady start. What I hadn't factored in, was the selfishness of some runners who had placed themselves too near the front, in time zones which were beyond them. This meant it was a slow, slow start like a herd of cattle. Too much overtaking and weaving from side to side, as people weren't running, and some as early as six and seven miles were walking. Although the plan was to trip along at 8mins per mile, in reality it was never on. Going through the first five miles in 43.00, and ten miles in 1hr 23, with hindsight I too perhaps should have started in a faster paced group. No real problems in the race as such, other than I developed a toe blister in Canary Wharf. The thing which bothered me the most was I'd accidentally stopped my wrist watch and my running time. So I had to do mental arithmetic every time I passed a timing station. The prospect of improving my time from '91 had disappeared, so just a case of trotting it home. I was a little disappointed at the time, as I finished full of running. What I was pleased about was my second half of the race was only 5 mins slower than the first.

Splits

5 miles	45.00
Halfway	1.50.00
21 miles	3.00.00
Time:	3.45.18

Marathon Post Script

After the usual slog through the crowds to find the baggage wagon, I set off to the nearest tube line to get out of town and back down to Ealing. This of course takes on a challenge of its own as one is tired, emotional and feeling a little sore in various places where Vaseline wouldn't reach. Still, finally back on to the district line I could at least sit down. What I failed to notice was the District Line West was a split line and instead of arriving in Ealing Broadway I was currently on route to Richmond. I then had to disembark at Gunnersbury to catch a train back, to then start my journey again. My repatriation with my van was such a relief.

Around 79,000 people applied to enter the race, of which 39,097 had their applications accepted and around 27,000 started the race. A total of 25,377 runners finished the race.

First Brit was Paul Evans in 5th place in a time of 2.10.31

Running Log

Event:	**Nelson 10 Suckley, Worcester**
Distance:	**10 miles**
Date:	**16th July**

I mention this race in memory of a dear old friend who passed in 2018, the one and only 'Ginger Plonker'. I'm unsure if this race still exists (I know the pub does) it is a beauty, surrounded by some lovely countryside. The race was organised twice a year, a summer version and a race on Boxing day over the same 10 mile course. The organisers were Cradley Heath AC (a fictitious running club only consisting of three members). Pete Farmer (Ginger Plonker), John Munchington, and another Brummie whose name escapes me.

Lots of lovingly crafted race signs adorned the route, Pete was nothing but a whizz at invention and had knocked up some imaginative race signs. 'Only one more hill to go and 'nearly halfway' were two I recall. My reward as ever was a decent pint after and a horse brass, which was the go-to reward around these rural race events.

Time: 70.50 Position: 28/56

FOR THE RECORD
Ceron seals second win

Dionicio Ceron retained his title in an enthralling race when he and Australian Steve Moneghetti hauled in and passed Antonio Pinto of Portugal in the closing stages after being over a minute down with 5 miles to go. Ceron and Moneghetti then ran together until they turned into The Mall where the Mexican surged to an unprecedented second victory in 2:08:30 – London's 2nd fastest time ever and only 14 seconds slower than Steve Jones' course record.

You had to feel sorry for Moneghetti, it was the second time in the race's history he had been beaten by 3 seconds. In 5th place Paul Evans ran 2:10:31, the fastest time of the year by a British athlete.

Sobanska sneaks home

The women's race was equally nail-biting. Three runners were together in the closing stages with favourite Manuela Machado of Portugal making much of the running. But it was Malgorzata Sobanska of Poland who made a decisive move and gained a 10 second lead which Machado, the European champion, was unable to close. Ritva Lemettinen of Finland finished 7 seconds behind Machado, who later that year went on to become World Champion, finished in 3rd.

Liz McColgan was the first Briton in 5th place. Still feeling her way back to full fitness after nearly three years of injury problems, she finished one ahead of Katrin Dorre, whose 3-year reign as champion finally ended.

Running Log

Event: **Forest of Dean Trail**
Distance: **Half Marathon**
Date: **Spring**

This was a relatively new (if not brand new event) being sponsored by Adidas who had put a marked /zoned trail course in the Cannop Ponds area.

```
Time: 1.34
     Position: 60/200
```

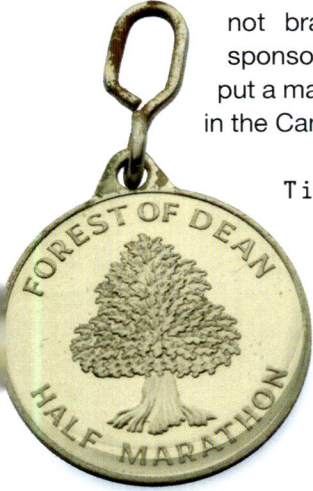

Running Log

Event: **Otmoor Challenge**
Distance: **Half Marathon**
Date: **Spring**

Historic Interest

Abingdon Arms is a lovely old pub with a fine garden affording great views across Otmoor. The arms in question are of James Bertie (1653 -1699) who was created 1st Earl of Abingdon in 1682. The Bertie family owned the village until 1919 when it was broken up and sold off in lots. The pub itself has a small bar area, with old photographs of the pub on display, and is dominated by a log fire in the big fireplace. There is a separate restaurant room. It is Grade II listed. Early C18. Apparently frequented by Lewis Carroll who may have got inspiration for the chessboard theme in 'Through the Looking-Glass' from the patchwork fields of Otmoor. Also regularly visited by Evelyn Waugh in the 1920s when he was an undergraduate and he now has a blue plaque.

The course itself runs around a RSPB wetland area Otmoor Nature Reserve. It passed its 40th Anniversary in 2019 and was set up to support all the seven villages. Registration is held at the impressive Horton Cum Studley, with the start and finish on the playing fields. But the best bit is the Féte which goes on simultaneously, complete with beer tent. Cut off field entry is around 300.

```
Time: 1.42.32 Position: 140/300
```

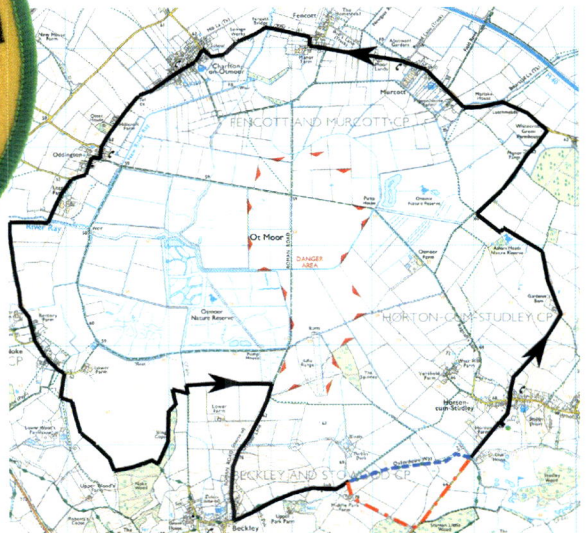

Running Log

Event: **Cleevewold**
Distance: **Cleeve Hill**
Date: **March**

Back for another crack at the Cheltenham Harriers attempt at a fell race. What a toughie. At least this year it was dry! Although I ran comfortably, I was a minute down on the last effort.

Time: 1.59.56

Running Log

Event: **Inter Hash, Limassol Cyprus**
Distance: **Varied**
Date: **7th-9th June**

A dose of the Mediterranean sun seemed too good an opportunity to miss, and so I signed up for the tenth Inter Hash in Cyprus. Registration for the weekend was again in a swanky hotel, this time the Mediterranean Beach Hotel in the Amathus area. On Friday tea time a steady queue of hashers had already gathered at the gates to Limassol's Municipal Gardens, where all the evening celebrations were to be based. Greek, or more accurately Cypriot, dancing wasn't really my thing, so I made a start on the mountain of Keo beer.

Saturday morning and a bazaar had sprung up in the gardens with tons of hash memorabilia, tee shirts and the like, which was a welcome distraction on the way to the bus area. A central terminus was situated right behind the gardens so was a perfect location. Eight hash trails were on offer and I plumped for Run 1, the Aphrodite Run. It was an area I knew and a relatively short journey out of town. Having said that, it was still a 3 hour procedure from boarding the bus to run site! hashers and buses continue to be a thorny problem.

Hash Trail 1 Melanda Beach
This one proved popular throughout the assembled pack, instead of being in running wear, more were dressed in, or clutching, beach wear. Today's Hares from Episkopi H3 were expecting 8 coach loads - instead 11 turned up! The run site and beach was found at the end of a bumpy track adjacent to the dual carriageway into Pathos. Cutting through an Orange grove and rock and scrub headland, down in the distance we could see the yellow and white Keo trucks bedecked with bunting.

Seeing the amount of hashers which had showed up, the Hares briefing contained some bad news. Instead of the anticipated 400 hashers, approximately 700 had arrived! Some emergency measures had to be put in place. "The scrub and bondu can take you all – that's no problem, but the beer may run low". Hey, no problem an Aussie had the answer: "NO BEER FOR THE SHEILAS!" So On On into the scrub and headland paths, it was arduous, arid and 'orrible.

Here was another Hash which used paper to mark the route. Shredded paper was placed on bushes so it wouldn't blow away, the hares then sweep the route and would collect it back up again. There was no real escape from the searing heat, as we dipped into ravines where the heat was trapped. There were only five checks the whole run, where as promised, each check held water and had a radio link. The run in was along the cliff top with the beer trucks shimmering in a heat haze below on the beach, but SCB at your peril - it was a steep drop.

The Apollo Run - Curium Stadium

The briefing began with history. This was the only ancient stadium found in Cyprus. The setting was an amphitheatre built in 200AD and could once seat 6,000 spectators. Importantly, it was the site of pentathlon events in ancient times, after the adjoining pantheon was destroyed by an earthquake and subsequent tsunami. What was incredible was just how far away the sea was from our vantage point, and later on in the run we would find en route some relics and ruins which had been washed inland.

Another set of Episkopi Hares had organised today's trail, and after the stern but reassuring brief we set off. It was across a powder dust of a track, some early farm land got a thorough examination where we found a water check in the shade of an orange grove. It then became all too familiar, rocky hillsides covered in JC*.

One memorable highlight of this trail was the regroup at a rubbish tip! A downward sweeping dirt track with a sheer drop on the one side, which was littered with abandoned TV sets, led the dehydrated pack towards the bottom of a ravine, where mercifully another water stop was laid on. Here we discovered those ancient relics I was on about. Moving off on trail, some tell-tale pylons came into view, now snaking through some vicious JC undergrowth, it was a lovely downhill finish to find the Keo truck

Inter Hash Party Night

As this particular Inter hash was in Europe it became a Brits' bash, certainly in conjunction with the home grown talents for cabaret (a loose term), with some near-the-knuckle mad-cap antics. I actually got roped into performing in a dance troop on stage in front of around 4000 hashers. A play on words - the Chippendales billed as the 'Chip N Ales' - nerve racking, but fun.

*JC = leafless dry dead plant with thorns on branches, which covers most outcrops all over Cyprus, and which hashers have nicknamed 'JC'. As when it catches your exposed flesh, you curse: Jesus Christ!

Running Log

Event: **Evesham Half Marathon**
Distance: **13 miles**
Date: **Bank Holiday Monday 5th May**

Running Log

Event: **Tewkesbury Half Marathon**
Distance: **13 miles**
Date: **Sunday 11th May**

Starting and finishing on Corporation Meadow, this was an ideal route to take in the Vales famous 'blossom' trail. The route soon leaves the town over the 'new bridge' and along Abbey Road before Cheltenham Road, turning sharp left to run parallel with the River Avon. The course then heads out into the market garden country side, well, at least its a flat course. The incident of the morning which has gone into folklore, and for any race organisers on what not to do.

After a fairly uninteresting stretch (main roads) we veered left at the Round of Gras public house (so named after the term used to bunch asparagus). The race was heading out towards the Littletons, but first had to cross the level crossing at Blackminster. This was around the 6 mile mark and the race had settled with the leading group of runners strung out in front. There is a small kink in the road slightly downhill before the road rises up to the unmanned level crossing. Arriving at the kink that unmistakable warning noise started to emit. Then the flashing lights and - you guessed it - down

came the barriers, allowing some 30–50 runners across the rail track. This left the rest of the field to bunch up against the barriers unable to cross as agonising minutes ticked by. Do we restart our watches? Some were tempted to sprint for it. Others just ran on the spot. What a cock up! It was rerouted the following year.

Time: 1.34.16

Being my local race the whole club (Tewkesbury AC) were encouraged to participate. Get the Gold and Black out on the streets, or something like that. Due to bad planning it was my second half marathon that week! Bredon, the village I was then living in, featured around the 7–8 mile distance. My two young sons were terribly disappointed I wasn't first past the end of our road leading the race! And had become very 'restless' as I finally plodded by.

Time: 1.39.16

Running Log

Event:	**Flora London Marathon**
Distance:	**26.2 miles**
Date:	**Sunday 13th April**

My preparation was lacking through Injury, I had been struggling with a dodgy left knee. I was determined not to miss out another year, so having not run for two weeks, I went for a six miler on the Wednesday before the Sunday to 'test' the knee. It seemed fine so decided to go for it.

Of course this was risking a breakdown smack bang in the middle of the race. In the first miles my worst fears were raised when my left knee and hip started to give me gip. Thankfully, by the time I'd rounded the Cutty Sark, it had eased. My problems - although I didn't know it - were further up the road.

Things were ticking along quite nicely by now. Over Tower Bridge, always a great lift, but then the ball of my right foot started to burn. I had to stop and inspect the damage. It was a blood blister. I had to stop several times after that and alter the sock position. That wasn't the worst of it, because I was clearly 'favouring the right' to avoid pressure on my weaker left injured side.

Even the awful pull along the highway - at least there were runners still going the opposite way and had the Dogs loop still to do - I skipped across the cobbles when I ran it in 1983 (we didn't have such luxuries as a carpet, what a treat on the knees).

I stopped along the Embankment (how I hate that stretch) and got chatting to a St Johns Ambulance lady as I pulled over for more running repairs. A wave to Big Ben as I passed by on my way to Buck House. I was in no hurry, I'd started and I was going to finish.

At 15 miles I pulled my right thigh and the quad got very sore towards the finish. However, for all this I really enjoyed my run. I was just happy to be running - it's a wonderful feeling jogging along with humanity as if you own the streets of London for a day.

Time: 3.45.18

How did Ralph McTell put it?

> *"So how can you tell me you're lonely,*
> *and say for you that the sun don't shine?*
> *Let me take you by the hand and lead you*
> *through the streets of London.*
> *I'll show you something to make you*
> *change your mind."*

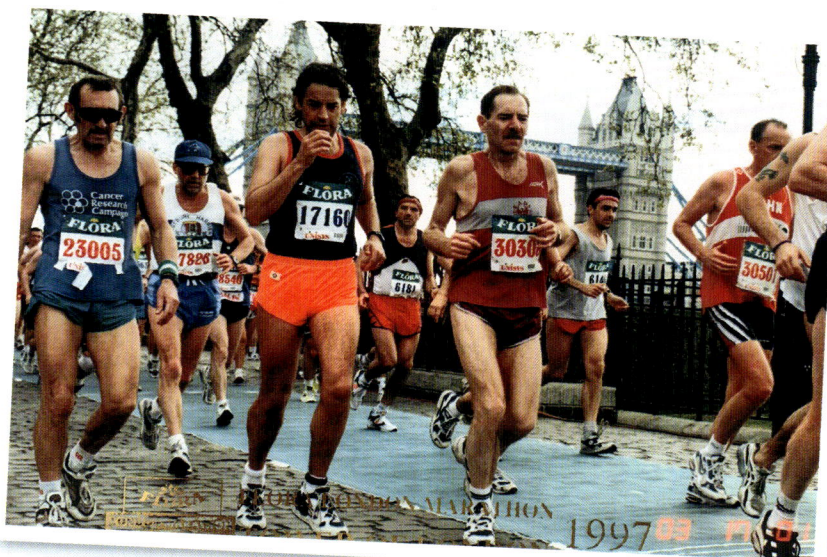

FOR THE RECORD
Pinto snatches victory and record

Steve Jones' 12 year old course record was finally eclipsed, but it took a race of the highest quality in which the winner was in doubt until the final strides. Antonio Pinto, one of the world's most consistent marathoners, came from way back over the final miles to snatch victory from the 1996 world half marathon champion, Stefano Baldini, winning in 2:07:55 to the Italian's 2:07:57. Josiah Thugwane of South Africa, the 1996 Olympic champion, was 3rd in 2:08:06, two seconds in front of Kenyan Erick Kimaiyo. Both Africans also beat Jones' former course record.

At 18 miles, when Baldini – after steadily working his way to the front – slipped into the driving seat, the main pack started to fragment and Pinto drifted out of the first five places. From then on all three leaders, Baldini, Thugwane and Kimaiyo, were pushing into uncharted territory. The Italian was on course to set a national record, the South African to miss his country's mark by just two seconds, and the Kenyan to remove 1:39 from his best.

At 23 miles, Britain's Richard Nerurkar rejoined the leading trio and then fell off the pace again. He was re-caught by a resurgent Pinto who then gathered in Kimaiyo and chased after the pair in front. Thugwane was eventually prised loose by Baldini between 25 and 26 miles but the Italian then had to contend with Pinto. After 26 miles both runners displayed incredible reserves of strength as they sprinted for the line with 1992 champion Pinto proving both faster and stronger. 8 of the first 10 set personal bests.

The women's race
Chepchumba gets her revenge

There was another glorious scrap in The Mall at the end of the women's race between Kenya's Joyce Chepchumba and Britain's Liz McColgan.

After Kenyan pacemaker Lornah Kiplagat led the field to halfway in 1:13:30, the 11-strong lead pack was tested by Sonja Krolik, a convert from triathlon. The 24 year old German slowly opened a gap that extended to 52 seconds by 20 miles. However, by 21 miles the gap was down to 28 seconds and with about 3 miles to go, Chepchumba and Lidia Simon of Romania passed Krolik.

At this point McColgan looked laboured and destined for 3rd place at best. But the Scot's supporters began to get excited as she fought her way up to Chepchumba and started a long drive for home as they turned off the Embankment. Crowd hysteria reached fever pitch as she entered The Mall. Liz, who won last year, was beaten after an amazing finish, just missing out on the £55,000 prize purse for the fastest woman. She sprinted shoulder to shoulder down the Mall with Kenyan Joyce Chepchumba, but lost out by a second. McColgan in 2:26:51. 6 of the top 10 women ran faster than ever before.

If the Race finish wasn't dramatic enough - Liz McColgan who had literally lost her marathon crown - then gave away her medal. Just minutes after her disappointment, big-hearted Liz put the gong round a young girl's neck in the crowd.

Running Log

Event:	**Midsummer Footpath Dream**
Distance:	**18 miles**
Date:	**June 1997**

Most runners would have heard of the Grizzly. A mammoth cross-country event ran in March - a real endurance event - over 18 miles often set in wet and cold conditions. However, once upon a time here was a summer event, organised by the same Axe Valley crew setting out from Seaton.

It seems inadvertently I had a hand in the Axe Valley being founded. Further back in the mists of time Dung Beetle (Hash name), remembers a post-run speech I gave on the virtues of the Hash House Harriers, the enjoyment and pleasure experienced from following a trail, and the accomplishment of completing it. Not to mention the warm glow of camaraderie with those who have shared the same experience back in the bar. This stayed with him and was the basis and ethos of the Axe Valley Runners.

That was kinda nice to hear, but I have no claim on this wacky idea for a race, but of course it appealed to me. The course distance was roughly eighteen miles. Nobody knew for sure the distance, but what they did know was that the route included six pub stops and a cream tea. Maybe more a Mad Hatters tea party, rather than a Shakespeare Midsummers dream!

The race was set in some wonderful East Devon countryside, whose terrain provided most surfaces along the route, from Beach to Moor. The race started on the Esplanade and was heralded with a sharp chilling rain shower whipping in off the sea. Along the Esplanade we had a small beach section before turning inland up a sharp incline (Castle Hill), before dropping back down to find the coastal path. This ran over White Cliff with stunning views on our left of the Seaton Bay below.

The coastal path dropped down through the Jubilee Memorial Gardens, where the route brought us out right opposite The Anchor pub. Where here, appropriately, our first beer was taken in Beer. My beer was waiting for me,

an extra entrance fee was charged to cover the refreshments. It was a swift half I downed and rejoined the race, it appeared some were on the additional option of beer and cream tea, while others were taking it more serious and just doing the run option only.

From the Anchor a steep lane (Common Lane) had to be climbed before the route traced the coastal path once more. The route rounded Beer Head, where now beautiful Branscombe could be seen in the distance. Pub no. 2 was the Fountain Head where a beer festival was already in full swing. It was very difficult leaving that scenario behind, all my will power was required.

The course now swung inland where a maze of Devon lanes zigzagged our way up to the A3052, where near Hangmans Stone, was situated pub no 3, the Three Horseshoes. After another swift half I rejoined the race route, but soon discovered I was on my own. Any pockets of runners whether in front or the rear had now disappeared. Still I jogged along merrily. The route continued inland towards Blackberry Camp, an Iron Age Hill fort, and this area was quite magical, running around and through its ancient ramparts.

On past and onto a gentle sloping lane, the first tarmac I'd encountered for a while. Up ahead I could see a lady Marshall offering water and encouragement. As I approached her; drinks and race straight on, cream teas left. So they weren't joking!

So I sat at a table with a Gingham tablecloth and china, in a lovely garden surrounded by a white picket fence while a waitress brought over my tea and scones and took a note of my race number. It was most bizarre. Not even Dali would've painted the scene. From here I'm not sure what happened next, but after leaving the table and sent off in a vague direction – I get lost. I blame the tea and scones, not the beer, although I wasn't the only one.

Coming in the other direction and looking flustered was a young teenager who I discovered was Heather, she was lost too and part of the more serious race group (No Beer, No Cream Teas)

Holding a wet finger up to the wind we headed off. It transpired we'd ran about a mile in wrong direction. We startled a holiday caravan park owner with our desperate pleas to tell us which was the right way to Colyton. We eventually made our way back, though the parish of Southleigh, and down into Colyton to get back on course, and where I found my next pub. Pub no. 4, The Kingfisher. I explained the situation to Heather and nipped in for a recharging half pint. Suitably refreshed I emerged into the warm afternoon sunshine once more. Heather was waiting for me. Just as well I think, as she made an excellent pace maker as we followed flat grassy meadows on towards Colyford and Pub no. 5, the White Hart.

We'd clocked up around 16.5 miles by now. I said to Heather to carry on as I disappeared into another pub, leaving her with a look of disappointment on her face. Another delicious real ale which did make me 'slightly heady'. Suitably downed, on on once more. I was really enjoying it now with still another pub to go. To my surprise, Heather was still dutifully waiting for me, she was still not confident of the route or felt some sense of responsibility for me (I did find her lost in the woods). Whatever, we ran on together or rather I tried to keep up with her, chatting as we went. The last pub was a classic CAMRA favourite in its guide for years on end. Pub No. 6, the Harbour Inn, a 12th Century beauty.

The run ended as it started, in a rain shower, it's about a mile along the front to the finish in Seaton, where Heather again led me across the finish line outside the Hook and Parrot. A hug and she was gone, looking as fresh as when she started!

Running Log

Event: **Advent Adventure**
Distance: **10 miles**
Date: **7th December 1997**

This was a Gloucester AC organised club event staged over Robinswood Hill. A country park and nature reserve since 1972, accessed just off the city ring road near Matson. Its' take up was from mainly local runners with the emphasis to beat the Gloucester boys (and girls). Quite a hilly route (undulating) which took in all sides of the hill in a figure of eight format. It was a tough ten mile course and I was thankful as I came around the smooth lines of the golf course back to the finish. Formed in 1995 the race ran for seven years.

Time: 73.06   Position: 37 /84

Years later I found out that Heather (Fell) turned out to be a serious pentathlete. She enjoyed success at junior level, including two gold and one silver medal in the 2003 World Junior Championships in Athens, representing GB. Then going on in the 2008 Summer Olympics to win the silver in the woman's modern pentathlon individual. She then retired and turned her hand to Triathlon. I wonder if she remembers our run?

Origins of The Red Dress Run

Alvin Stardust had a hit record with 'Red Dress' back in the 1970s, and while I must confess to actually buying this record with my pocket money, little did I know that I would be wearing one, at least in public! Throughout my recollections I mention the infamous Red Dress Run so perhaps a brief explanation may be in order.

A trio in Red for Warwick H3 RDR. With the much missed Hubcabs.

On August 7, 1987, a young lady wearing a red dress emerged from an aeroplane that had landed in southern California to visit a friend from her high school years. Shortly thereafter, she found herself transported to Long Beach, where her friend introduced her to a zany running group called the 'Hash House Harriers'. Donna Rhinehart was the Lady in Red.

The GM, noting her attire, invited her to wait in the Beer Truck until the pack returned, but Donna had other ideas, and ran the trail in dress and heels. The following year (August 12, 1988), to commemorate the event, the San Diego Hash House Harriers sent 'The Lady In Red' an airline ticket to attend the inaugural Red Dress Run. In addressing the crowd, The Lady In Red suggested that Hash House Harriers hold the Red Dress Run annually as an occasion to be used to raise funds for local charities.

The tradition of the Hash House Harriers Red Dress Run quickly spread to every corner of the globe, including Beijing, Montreal, Ho Chi Minh City, Helsinki, Moscow, Tokyo, Washington DC, Hobart (Australia) and countless other locations. Over the years, the Red Dress Run has been very successful in raising millions of dollars/pounds for a wide variety of local charities. For example, the New Orleans Hash House Harriers attracted 7,000 participants to their Red Dress Run in 2010, raising more than $150,000 for 50 local charities.

Donna passed away in 2013, but her legacy lives on on... Today the Red Dress Run is an integral part of the Hash House Harriers' heritage and has become the curtain raiser to the UK's Nash Hash Weekends. It is every bit iconic as the Royal Selangor Club where the Hash House Harriers were born, and as sacred as our founder Gispert's Drinking Vessel.

1998, 1999, 2000, 2001 - Four Fallow Years

From a fairly consistent trail of running, over the next few years my competitive edge petered out as any regular training sessions or interest in running events took a back seat, my training dairies became redundant of course, as it coincided with the little introduction of my two sons, Jared and Craig. As a consequence it resulted in a six year gap from racing, but my running continued, generally only with the Hash House Harriers. Incidently, a few years previous, I had discovered the joy of mountain biking and so went racing those instead. Inspired by the emerging sport, I started a MTB club, a social based group entitled the CRANKS. (Cheltenham Rides And Never Konsiders Stopping) The club is still cycling regularly although I don't go along these days.

As life does, I encountered a few challenges over the next few years. My marriage broke up, and with my youngest son Craig contracting Meningococcal Septicaemia (which put him in intensive care, mercifully to survive), but several years of hospital stays and skin grafts followed. He now runs his own gardening and landscaping company.

Living in the village of Bredon, I soon got immersed in local activities, included adopting a football team to coach. After a few years coaching grass roots village junior teams, I went on several FA coaching courses progressing to taking my badges, I gained an UEFFA B badge (now called level 3), which resulted in me coaching in Birmingham Cities Youth and Juniors for a while, before joining Worcester City and running teams in the Midland Junior Premier.

The Midland Junior Premier was a league set up for non-professional teams who run academies at U/14-U/16 level. From this experience I was co-opted into setting up a new Stroud FC which was an exciting project, and offered some good experiences and helped a few overlooked youths who didn't quite make it into the local professional set ups.

In 2003 I also started my own printing business, in Tewkesbury. So any spare time was a rarity to go running.

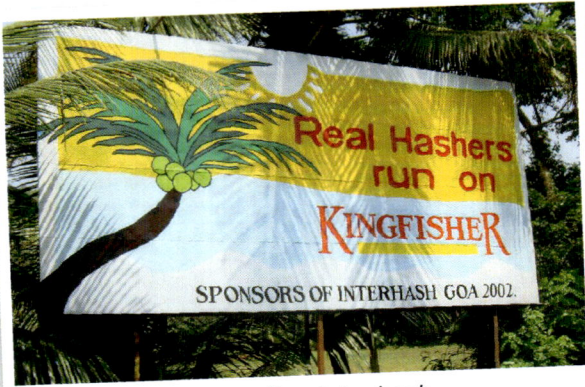

A Warm Welcome to Goa Inter hash

The Open Air Party Tent – Goan Style (Worked a treat until the monsoon season broke on the closing night)

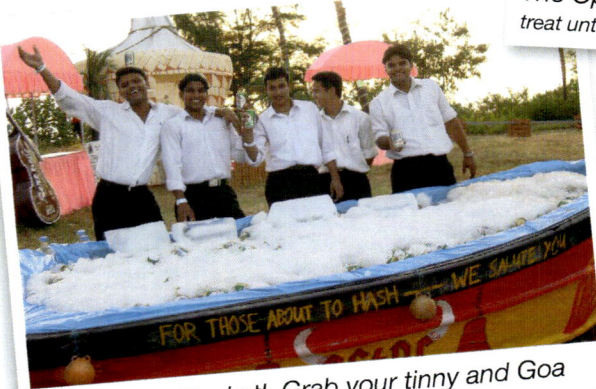

What an Ice Bucket! Grab your tinny and Goa

On On past - Our Lady of Immaculate Conception Church.

Basilica of Bom Jesus

Running Log

Event: **Inter Hash Goa India**
Distance: **Varied**
Date: **27 to 29 September (Att: 2600+)**

It was back in the late 1960s when the hippies and back-packers started to search out the tranquil and calming effect of the southern Indian state of Goa. It wasn't so laid-back when the hash turned up in town in late September of 2002. It wasn't the first invasion of course, Vasco da Gama was the Portuguese captain who first landed in Goa in 1498.

India, especially the Beach Resort of developing Goa, was an ideal location to put on an Inter Hash, with thousands of western visitors pouring in to fill the local coffers. Back in 2002 Goa was still undeveloped and certainly maintained that hippy vibe and laid-back approach. This was typified on the Friday curtain raiser, normally a Red Dress Run, where although a Charity fund raiser (for local charities) all participants have to wear Red Dresses, there is a run! On this occasion it was a Yellow Dress Parade! Starting at Donna Paula, the walk took in the streets of Panjim, Goa's state capital, the highlight (apart from the football ground) was passing the baroque Our Lady of Immaculate Conception Church.

The weekends' main hub where the events of Inter Hash were being hosted was due south, at the Old Anchor, Cavelossim, Here a huge system of marquees had been erected, including an old farts' tent - where I seemed to spend most of my evenings it must be said. Here you meet the doyens of World hash, and (if you get them early enough), a lot of insight and history can be gleaned from such conversations. Also encouragement to get involved in shaping hash events. Certainly at home in the UK it was also a bit quieter and the beer was easier to get to.

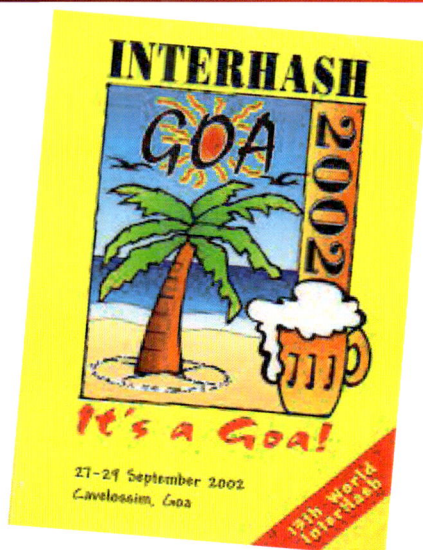

INTERHASH
GOA 2002
It's a Goa!

27-29 September 2002
Cavelossim, Goa

13th World InterHash

In truth, the hash runs weren't up to much. Being a satellite venue, with no local hash's recces and planning, it was very ad-hoc and last minute. Many started in bush, lush green with shaded clearings and ended on beach fronts, or vice versa.

The runs I managed were concentrated in Old Goa itself, and were fascinating, as much of the architecture was left over from when Goa was a Portuguese colony. The trails ran into jungle along red brick clay paths. Crumbling white stone washed hamlets sprung up from nowhere where we checked out various routes cheered on by Indian street urchins. We often uncovered mosaics amongst the overgrown abandoned settlements. The real treat.

These were relics of course from the Portuguese. From 1510 the Portuguese looked to gain control of the spice route from the East. As a result In 1542 the Jesuit missionaries followed, led by St Francis Xavier.

Incredibly his preserved body still lies in the Basilica of Bom Jesus in the square of Old Goa. Every ten years it is placed on public display inside the Church which coincided with my stay so I was able to queue up and witness his shrine. Hashing really does place you in situations and give you moments you would never experience without.

GLASGOW MARATHON
2327
1987

NIKE
GLASGOW HERALD

IAAF/ADT
World
Marathon
Cup 91

T and J Printers (UK) 0604 744200
6531

Uncle Ben's
1994 Polytechnic Marathon
86

adidas®

BITTON ROAD RUNNERS
788
EASY RUNNER

ROGUE
233
233
RUNS

THE MANDY WHITTINGTON
SPARES · GARDEN · TRACTION
NEWENT 9
246
Printed by RUNNING IMP LTD · 01522 502131 · www.runningimp.co.uk

Wye Valley Brewery
MUDDY WOODY 6
288

Running Log

Event:	**Inter Hash Cardiff - Wales**
Distance:	**9 miles**
Date:	**23-25 July (Att: 4549)**

So after a few exotic locations, Inter hash comes to the UK, more accurately Wales, and the Principality City of Cardiff. Most of the trails (runs) were held away from the city, and most of the buses and coaches of Wales were tied up for the weekend. With destinations as far as the Forest of Dean, or a bucket and spade trip to Porth Cawl, the organisers did their best to showcase what Wales had to offer. The curtain raiser on such an event is the Red Dress Run: a charity fund raiser where traditionally the runners all had to don those Red Dresses.

Instead, I chose a more low-key event and went along to an Indonostalgia Hash run. This is a part-time hash group running just twice a year with the accent heavily on hash experience of hashing in Indonesia. The hares try to import Bintan beer and insist on a Makan Supper. The Red Dress run was from the Vulcan, an historic Cardiff hostelry.

The run itself was unremarkable, a whistle-stop tour of inner city thoroughfares and back alleys. Only the pub was memorable along with the Brain's beer, and the old hash sweats that turned up in this downtown relic.

Welsh Weekend

All the Evening entertainment was held in the Magnificent Millennium Stadium along with the food booths and beer points.

For the Saturday Hash trail I choose to take part in the Welsh Valleys Hash. Around a 9 miler, it started somewhere near Pontypridd. As you would imagine it was made up of steep climbs, some forestry and the odd disused mine shaft or two. Making your way up and over Mynydd Y Cymmer was tough, but it had a beauty to this windswept wilderness. Dropping into the Rhondda Valley was also a shock to the senses, as grey and lifeless heaps of slag coloured your trainers, and socks took on nice black soot colour. While in the distance what looked like child's Lego thrown down the stairs was in fact, the neat rows of terraced houses which line the sides of the valley.

Each house had been painted different to the next. The houses of the Rhondda were built for the miners of the local colliery which has now closed of course, the last being Mardy Colliery in 1990. The On On with packed lunches and beer was held at Tonypandy.

The Rhondda Valley - to coin a phase: "I know, 'cos I was there!" (apologies to M Boyce).

Tucked away down a side street between the Railway station (Queen Street) and the Gaol, it was once a very grubby, **well-used** pub for the working classes. On my visit much of the area had been wiped away with new development, all around the sad old Vulcan. Although voted Cardiff Pub of the Year by the local branch of CAMRA in both 1997 and 2009, the writing was on the wall, as Brains confirmed they were terminating the licence.

The Vulcan - in all its former glory

A local campaign sprung up and gained a stay of execution, as a result of a petition that was raised that gathered over 5,000 signatures. Politicians were lobbied, and celebrities including band member James Bradfield of the Manic Street Preachers, also actor Rhys Ifans. However, time was called in 2012 finally with the building again facing demolition. Again a howl of protest was heard and somehow with local finance an agreement

The 'strip' - brick by brick

was made to donate the building to the St Fagans National Museum of History. So in July 2012, building contractors and preservationists were deployed by the National History Museum to start deconstruction of the building by hand, to allow brick by brick movement to St Fagans. The eventual plan is to reopen the pub with a suitably-styled historic theme, with actors serving historic ales. The opening was due in 2019/2020, but Covid delayed this date.

Many years on, the pub has been meticulously reconstructed to look as it did in 1915. From the original bricks and like-for-like replica of the tiled frontage, to sawdust spread across the floor and its bright orange urinals, no detail has been overlooked. The only difference is that it's got a new home on the grounds of Cardiff's St Fagans National Museum. Officially The Vulcan officially reopened as a working pub on 11 May 2024.

I had missed the enjoyment of racing - the sense of battle against a course or fellow competitor - especially if you could give them a year or two. Of course, getting back into racing (more like cruising I called it), was hard.

Age, and a relatively sedate period allows a few extra pounds to grip on. I still had a fondness for the off-road and multi-terrain events, so knocked off the dried mud and ventured off to a few local events.

Running Log

Event:	**Woodchester MT8**
Distance:	**8.4 miles**
Date:	**September**

A Stroud & District AC organised event in the grounds of the National Trust, with the jewel being the Manor house which you sweep by twice. Once after the long, long downhill on a Cotswold stone-strewn track, and again on the long, long climb back out of the valley. In between, the route takes in some vicious climbs along fire roads and tracks, where the scenery is magnificent.

Perhaps, now cruising instead of racing, I can now enjoy these sights. Woodchester Manor is an unfinished Gothic Mansion stuck in the bottom of a Cotswold valley. Unfinished because when William Leigh died no family members had their fathers' grandiose gothic aspirations or indeed the finance.

Time: 114.04   Position 97/119

Running Log

Event:	**Sodbury Slog**
Distance:	**10 miles**
Date:	**14th November**

Presented by Bitton Road Runners, The Sodbury Slog has quickly gained a reputation as a mud-fest not to be missed. It doesn't have the gimmicks of the Tough Guy, just honest-to-goodness cross country pain. It's another event not for the faint-hearted! Roads get overlooked, just mainly hills with strength-sapping mud. Numbers regularly attract over 1200 runners. Often oversubscribed, it is heralded by a sombre start, as the race always coincides with Remembrance Sunday, and is preceded by exhortation, a two minute silence and playing of the Last Post, which sets the scene for a memorable day. The Slog uses the same paths, fields, ditches and mud baths since it's original inception in 1990.

Time: 2.27 Position: 501/902

GLC
Gillette
LONDON MARATHON '83 ©

GLASGOW
MARATHON

THE OTMOOR CHALLENGE
7
TOWNS
1991

AOT LONDON
1991
MARATHON
Reebok OLYMPUS

WHITBREAD READING HALF MARATHON
10th YEAR
1992

THE OTMOOR CHALLENGE
7
TOWNS
199

Seven Sisters
MARATHON

Running Log

Event: **Dursley Dozen**
Distance: **12 miles**
Date: **20th February**

This multi-terrain staple was in its sixteenth year, and is a real roller-coaster of a run, scaling most if not all the hills surrounding the tight Dursley town area. The race started outside the Old Spot Inn, which means a steep uphill pull up the lane until you reached the Golf course (Stinchcombe) - exposed, but at least flat - then the course ran around the perimeter. Woods above Waterley Bottom, with plenty of mud thrown in, made up part of the course, plus a loop through the aptly named Break Heart Quarry.

Time: 1.58.00   Position: 267/380

Running Log

Event: **Gloucester 20**
Distance: **20 miles**
Date: **6th March**

Held in Frampton-on-Severn, a rural village south of the city, it offers quiet country roads to do the distance, starting on The Green, said to be the longest in Europe. The course heads out towards Saul and Upper Framilode. It's generally a flat route which is where at Epney and Longney an anti clockwise loop is run twice.

Time: 3.12.35   Position: 412/476

Running Log

Event: **Chedworth Roman Trail 10**
Distance: **10 miles**
Date: **3rd April**

This was a birthday treat (or rather the promise of a slap-up meal in the Seven Tuns after). This was a final tweak of what preparation I had in the tank for the up-coming London Marathon. Starting from the Village Hall it is a beauty of a route taking in the Coln Valley and Stowell Park. It is challenging, as Cotswold hills are steep! It of course runs close to the famous Chedworth Roman Villa.

Time: 1.31.13   Position: 180/315

The Hash has developed a new shape in super athletes.

Running Log

Event: **FLORA London Marathon**
Distance: **26.2 miles**
Date: **17th April (25th Anniversary)**

This was the quarter of a century marathon, a much-heralded event for which the organisers had lined up a stunning entry. This was an occasion I felt would be good to be part of, and much to my surprise, I managed to sneak an entry.

It was some eight years since I last pitched up on the start line. I hadn't realised at the moment I received my entry, but I think my marathon days were behind me. However, my eldest son has developed an interest in running and had become a Cheltenham Harrier. Dad spent many evenings at the Prince of Wales Stadium in Cheltenham, watching Jared being put through his paces. The weekend of the London Marathon was his 15th birthday, and what a great way to celebrate we thought. Yeah, Right! Some training and indeed some preparation races were taken in, but I simply didn't have that bedrock of mileage that is required to tackle a marathon with reasonable success. Staying in Earls Court so we could make a weekend of it, also it meant that an eager boy could take in the Marathon exhibition at the Excel Arena, plus a slap-up birthday meal in a swanky restaurant in Chelsea.

An over-indulgence of wine there didn't help my efforts the following morning. It was an uncomfortable run, certainly from 15 or 16 miles. My pace was consistent going through 10k in 59.01 and 20k in 1.58.17. I was under-trained, but got over Tower Bridge and through halfway in 2.04.53, but it was all downhill after that. Looking back, it was a momentous day taking part in what was the race's 25th Anniversary and the day Paula Pooped.

Time: 4.28.21
Position: 18127 / 35195

Highways and Byways

Who knows how quicker Paula may have been if she hadn't taken that unscheduled pitstop? Ironically, the ladies marathon champion got into difficulties along the Highway stretch, some 4 or 5 miles out from the Mall and its finish line. I say ironic, as in a cruel twist of fate, that Roman road was originally known as Ratcliffe Way. The name 'Ratcliffe' literally means 'red cliff', referring to the red sandstone cliffs which once descended from this plateau. To avoid flooding, the Roman road was built up from the Wapping Marshland in the south. The Highway was a terrible area, full of vice and crime, very seedy and downtrodden. One of Charles Dickens' favoured opium dens was along the Highway.

So as stomach cramps became too much, and with a healthy lead, she dashed to the side of the road along Tower Hill. This didn't do much to restore the former fabled shady area.

Marathon Baggage Reclaim

FOR THE RECORD

The men's race – which included the current Olympic and world champions, the world record holder and world all-time number 2 – followed the pattern of recent years with a large and extremely talented pack prowling behind the pacemakers until well past the half-way mark.

The repeated changes of pace eventually broke up the large pack and Italy's Stefano Baldini, the Olympic champion, was among those to be cut adrift, along with Britain's Jon Brown, 4th in that very same Olympic race. At 10k, the leading group had numbered 19, by half way reached in 63:22, it was down to 9 plus the two pacemakers.

Martin Lel's pace first killed off Rutto and Korir, reducing the pack to 4. Then Tergat was in trouble and, with the medals decided, it was just a matter of who got which colour. At 20 miles Tergat had told Lel to "Push, push!", and that is exactly what he did over the last 5km. So it was. Lel came home in 2:07:26, 23 seconds in front of Gharib with Ramaala crossing the line 43 seconds later. Running tough, Baldini and Brown came through in the closing stages for 5th and 6th places respectively, Brown setting a lifetime best of 2:09:31 to move him up to 12th on the British all-time list.

The women's race - London belongs to Paula
Paula Radcliffe's performance in 2005 was every bit as dominating as the previous two, banishing any lingering doubts she might have had after her 2004 Olympic disappointment. Her record in the London Marathon reads: 3 starts, 3 wins, 3 world records.

Having asked to be paced through the half-marathon mark in 68:30, Radcliffe dispensed with pacemaker services in the 5th mile and passed half way alone in 68:27. Paula's intentions were clear from the start, she ran the first mile in 5:03 and already had clear road behind her. During miles 5 and 6 Paula made some slight but significant moves, and reached the Cutty Sark pulling away from the two Kenyans (Susan Chepkemei and Margaret Okayo).

At 15 kilometres she led by 28 seconds from Okayo who in turn was 19 seconds clear of Chepkemei. Interestingly. She continued to drive to wards the finish as only Plaua could. However at the 23rd mile, she suddenly swerved to the side of the road and stopped. The watching TV audience must have had

flashes of her Athens disaster – but 15 seconds later she set off again. Explaining the incident after the race, she said "I had stomach problems at around 16 miles and I should have 'gone' before I did, but I didn't want to resort to that in front of thousands of people."

Suitably relieved, Paula continued pushing against the wind, completely unaware of her 4 minute plus lead because of the crowd noise. "They were so loud in places I thought I would be deafened", she said. Radcliffe came home to yet more delirious cheering, 1 minute and 14 seconds faster than her women-only world record.

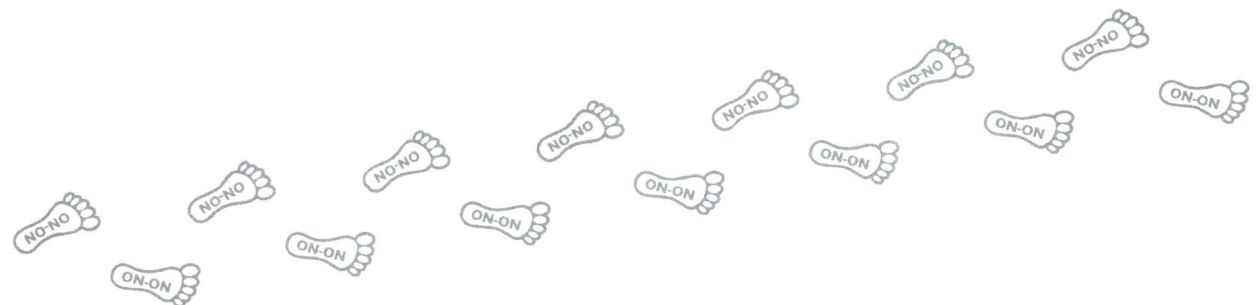

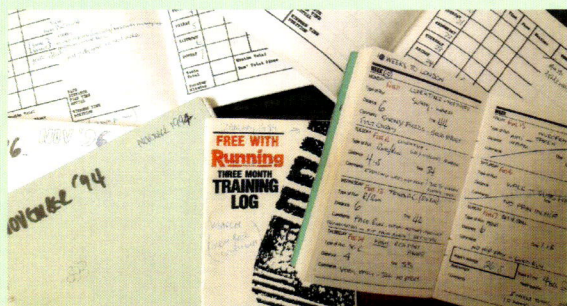

INJURIES

I hadn't thought of including an Injuries column - that would be dull wouldn't it? But recovering from injuries is part and parcel of a runner's life and we've all suffered that height of agony of trying to run faster or further, to when injury strikes, just being able to run again. Aah, the paradox.

Over-use injuries are the main problem generally, especially with club runners. However, whilst going back through my training dairies and with twenty years of hindsight, some rational explanations reveal just why I spent so many weeks in the Sports Injuries Clinic.

Training of course requires repetitive bouts of running and for everyone as mentioned, the overuse injury. If you don't already keep a running diary, I would recommend it. You don't need to be Samuel Peeps or get too scientific, although with wrist watch technology these days that is easier to accomplish. Logging the mileage and timings of course are a key component, but so are the injury indicators. That sore knee that started on your way home, the calf that just aches. If you log these you can pinpoint and perhaps head off a full-blown injury before it strikes.

Mentioned at the beginning of the book is an account of my first half marathon, which was accomplished in a pair of squash shoes. As many of my contemporaries in the 80s we had very little in protective or supportive footwear I remember one runner (I'll spare him his shame), he used to run in bri-nylon brown socks). Hi-Tech Silver Shadow was a popular trainer of choice. An early Nike I used to favour was the Internationalist, until the Nike Pegasus came along in 1983.

My list of Injuries is quite comprehensive. Are you ready for a touch of Latin?
• Iliotibial band – both knees
• Trochanteric bursitis
• Pica syndrome – left knee
• Soleus - right calf
• Gastrocnemius - right calf
• Plantar fasciitis – right foot
• Pes Anserinus Burstitis (Goose foot)
• Right Knee
• Hamstrings

During the early years of my running and training I ran into trouble a lot, and frustratingly was bounding along one minute, and limping and in agony the next. This meant I frequently missed weeks of training and prep before many a big race which I'd hoped to run well in. I'm not sure if marathons are quite the vogue that they were, it seems many have faltered or entries bombed, giving organisers a headache over finance. The obvious race to buck the trend continues to be the London Marathon. So, after several 'spoilt attempts' at training properly for the marathon I switched to a low mileage - long run strategy in an attempt to stay injury free. It worked only moderately as I was often undercooked for races.

Fast forward to (yet) another Physio Visit

I am now armed with some relatively new information and an insight as to why I was so injury prone. Looking back at my entries 'sore hip after hilly run' and another entry 'outside pain of left knee goes after a couple of miles' very sore next day.' I still run regularly and still enjoy the freedom it gives, and while not 'competing' any more, I still get injured regularly – or did. Back in 2016 I had new injury problem: Plantar Fasciitis, and whist I home cured before, this was proving tricky to shift.

After explaining the issue, the physio got me to whip off my shoes and socks and I was asked to take a wander up the corridor. Within seconds: "Yep, I can see the problem – you have one leg shorter than the other". Really?! I couldn't believe it. After all those hours in a rehab not once had a physio thought to look at the root cause. It was something so simple. I still get injured of course, but armed with podiatry inserts, it's helped enormously.

Running Log

Event: **EDF Birmingham Half Marathon**
Distance: **13.1 miles**
Date: **11th October 2009**

I'd always like Brum. The grubby and decaying warehousing left over from the Industrial age, along the overgrown canals, banks, even the graffiti, didn't put me off its charm. Of course this was back in the 1980s. Regeneration has smartened up the basins and wharfs and it's now a trendy area in Gas Street and Brinnley, with bars and restaurants, etc. I was reacquainted with the delights of Brum in the naughties when my eldest son Jared spent four years at Aston University.

Birmingham was a bit of a back-water, and when it came to mass participation marathons, the UK's second city, unlike any other, didn't have an established race. One did start up at the beginning of the 80s with the coincidence of the running boom.

The inaugural City of Birmingham Marathon was held on Sunday, 20th September 1981, and started at the NEC, running into the city centre and back. The following year, it morphed into 'The Peoples Marathon' for the next few years, before running out of steam. Inner city restructuring was blamed for its demise as Birmingham underwent a massive redevelopment programme, which meant a nightmare as road closures and general upheaval made it impossible to plot and establish a course. However, the marathon gave way for the Brum Fun Run had bowed out, starting and finishing at the Edgbaston Cricket Ground.

In 2008 a Half Marathon was reintroduced - The EDF Energy Birmingham Half Marathon - subsequently from 2011 it became part of the Great Run Series of races.

For 2009 my son suggested we sign up for the race as a sort of farewell to the city, as he'd finished and graduated from Aston. The cherry on the cake was the fact that it was an International field. As the city of Birmingham was selected for the World Championship race (men/women) by the IAAF Council, after a presentation by UK Athletics. It marked the return to a big city race in Birmingham. It was actually the third time the championships were held in Great Britain, following Newcastle in 1992 and Bristol in 2001.

A night out in the Bull Ring is always a good night out and the Malls and restaurants on the Saturday Night had that feel of a big race day, as you spot the runners and families, mainly in Italian Restaurants shovelling in the pasta.

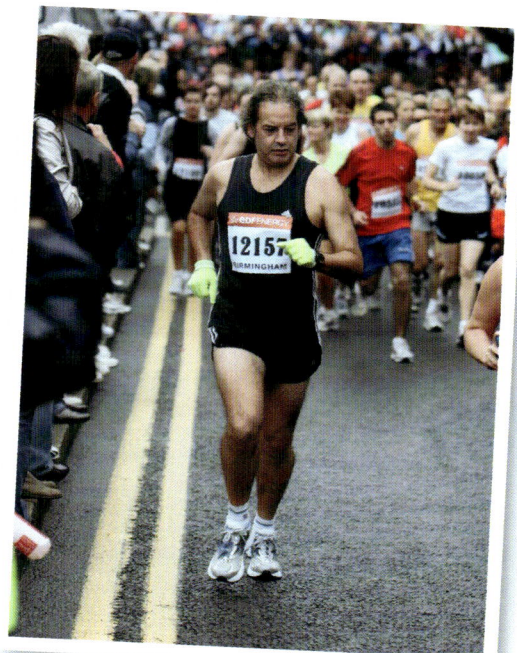

Kelly won both 800 metres and 1500 metres Gold at the Summer Olympics in Athens in 2004. The excellent wide thoroughfares took the masses away from the centre of town. The route was generally an out and back route, first making its way out to Cannon Hill Park.

Although we started together, Jared had made his way into a faster time zone, so I had no idea how he was getting on. The overcast sky had now released steady drizzle into our faces. The route took the runners out toward Cannon Hill Park before we ventured out to my favourite part of the course, Bournville Village. Really good crowd support here I remember, even if it was pouring down. The route was mainly flat with very few twists and turns, ideal I guess for a championship race and fast times.

Edging through Edgbaston it was a fast flat dash back into the centre of Brum where the course was strewn with huge puddles. I splashed my way back into town, first along the Hagley Road, then across the Fiveways roundabout. I was having a good run and in truth didn't mind the overcast and wet conditions, and was already beginning to look forward to my lunchtime pint in one of my favourite watering holes. Broad Street seemed to go on and on, as I think I missed-timed my sprint for the finish line. Eventually through the crowds I could spot the Bouton Watt and Murdoch statue and made that desperate, legs-of-jelly lunge for the line. Jared had a time of 1.52.00.

Time: 1.55.21

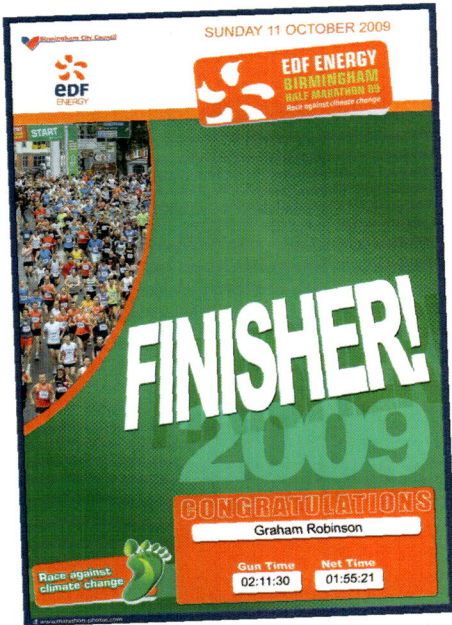

Race day dawned overcast as we gathered in the Millennium Square. The top Athletes of course lined up a good half an hour before the masses. The Start line was just opposite Symphony Hall on the corner of Bridge Street, where we filed past the 'official starter' for the event, Dame Kelly Holmes. Where I do admit I pushed and shoved my way across to her side of the road to give her a high five as I ran past.

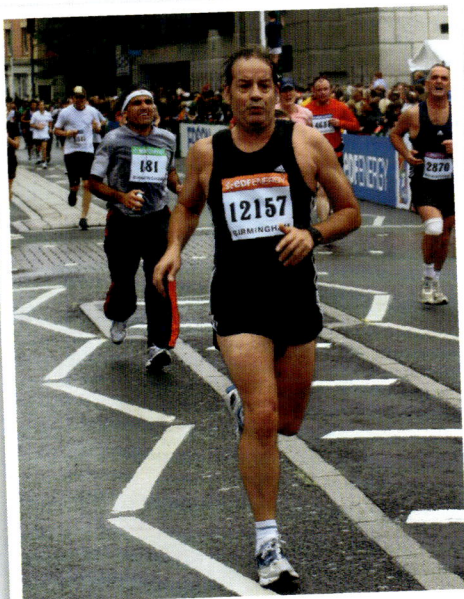

Eyes on the prize (the finish line)

Running Log

Event: **Birmingham Black Country Half**
Distance: **Marathon**
Date: **6th July**

After all these years of running I'm always on the lookout for something a bit novel and this event struck a chord with me. It's organised by Stuweb, an electronics timing company, for which the format of this event serviced them perfectly. It's a unique point-to-point course (A–B), with the start being in Wolverhampton running down the Birmingham canal into the City Centre.

The race is held early on a Saturday, so once runners have sorted out the logistics of leaving their cars in Birmingham, etc. it can be a bit hetic. For our visit an overnight was preferable which eliminated all that h a s s l e in the morning. Jules and I stayed in the Premier Inn which was adjacent to the mornings' start. It was a glorious summer evening on that Friday so not even bothering to change after our drive we threw in the cases and went to the adjoining pub – the Blue Brick. It was a typical new build pub, but it's in a conservation area and its name ties in with the former rail and waterways buildings. Known locally as the Union Mill Conservation Area, established in 1985.

Broad Street Basin is the starting area where many of the original buildings remain as does the surrounding streets which have blue engineering brick paving, hence the name. The Blue brick was thronged with competitors and the warm sunshine and atmosphere meant that we consumed more Stella Artios than was wise. Especially as the Saturday, as race day transpired to be the hottest day of the year. I did suffer some what in the latter stages.

The novelty is that the runners go off in staggered starts, generally in 30 second intervals where a pre-predicted time is feed into the data to place your starting position accordingly. It's a race or run where you have to be comfortable with your own company as you can run several miles without actually see anybody, except way in the distance. Canal paths can be narrow and very straight so mental strength is required to keep going when you hit a bad patch.

The infamous Corseley Tunnel is a highlight on the course - it's a dank, dark, 300 yard tunnel cut into the hillside. Except this year it was shut while repairs to land slippage took place. This meant we were diverted off the tow path up a steep hill to connect to the road at the top and then drop down some steep steps back to rejoin the path. The occasional canal-side pub is passed, but early on in the race, if had been around the 8 – 10 mile mark I would have pulled in. The route does 'kink' from time to time, and runs through some forgotten derelict industrial past. Tipton is quite an industrial area, as we move on down toward Sandwell and Smethwick.

Drink stations are placed every three miles which on this occasion became more and more vital as the sun was blistering. These were often placed on barge boats which was novel. Another feature, or eye sore dependant on your view, was as the canal disappears under the M5, huge concrete columns sunk in the Waterways to hold the road up! The route crosses over ornate bridges from time to time, the steep inclines becomes increasingly difficult. The finish line is in the heart of Brindley Place which makes for a tight finish, you can't actually see the gantry as the curve of the canal keeps it hidden until the last second. Its a great place to finish the event as the crowds are huge and the best bit Gas

Street Basin is just close to hand, full of bars and restaurants to celebrate the last thirteen miles. As mentioned its an A–B course, so Jules had waved me off in Wolverhampton, then jumped in the car and drove to Brum to cheer me home.
Time: 2.24.51   Position: 609

I enjoyed the novelty of this event so much that I went back another couple of times, such is the lure of the black country.

July 2nd 2016 Time: 2.17.57

July 1st 2017 My incentive this time around was its' tenth anniversary and participants' exclusive tee shirt.

Time: 2.17.57 Position: 826

Along the canal during a revisit in 2017

Running Log

Event: **Saltfest 9**
Distance: **9 miles**
Date: **13th September**

Organised by Droitwich Athletics Club, this event coincided with the towns' weekend festival, linked to their salt heritage. Starting from Vines Park, this unusual staggered start system drip-fed runners out onto the course in pairs at 20 second intervals. This is due to the course being narrow for the first mile or so. It follows the riverside walk before dovetailing into the Droitwich canal. Dipping under the M5 motorway and heading out to the Eagle & Sun pub, it then heads out along the Worcester & Birmingham. Predominately flat, save for the odd climb up a lock, it was some fine countryside to enjoy.

Once off the tow path we began to loop back, taking in the enormous climb up to St Mary the Virgin, a church perched on the top of a hill, which offered a panoramic view. After the climb, a nice downhill section - thank goodness - to Hanbury Hall and its neat grounds. The other unusual aspect about this race is it tucks back into the out route, so at least one could figure out how far you had left to run.

Time: 1.33.46 Position: 84/107

Running Log

Event: **Bull Run**
Distance: **4 miles**
Date: **25th October**

The Horton Bull Run began as a Fun Run in 1983 mainly to raise money for the local Village Hall. Some might remember Diana Moran, (aka the Green Goddess) who was a keep fit celebrity started the race. A lovely cross country chase through South Gloucestershire, taking in Hawkesbury and Horton Court, which has been used as a filming location for both Wolf Hall and Poldark.

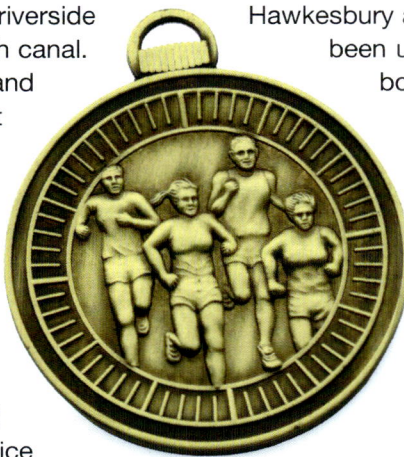

Time: 55.04
Position: 60/86

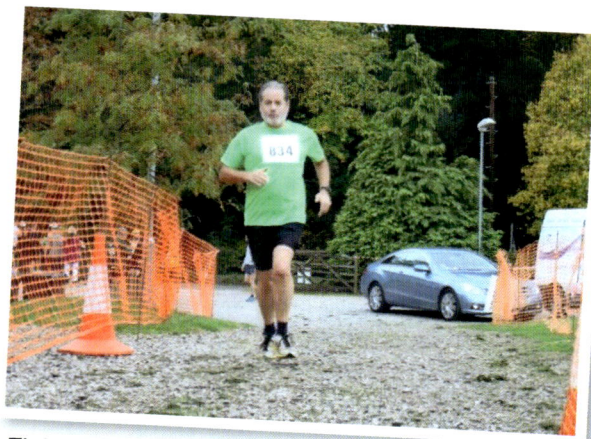

Finishing straight or builders yard?

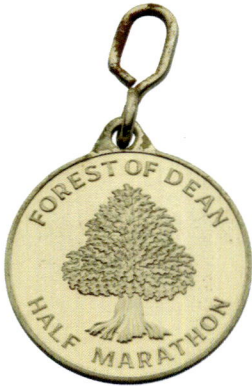

Running Log

Event: **Poets' Path**
Distance: **9 miles**
Date: **January**

Although this was the 8th staging, I only just discovered another quirky event in the rather attractive setting of Dymock. Its' organisers were a couple I'd met years before when they were members of Tewkesbury AC. Ed & Phil always had a passion for the outdoors and local history, in this case the Dymock Poets.

Shortly before the First World War, a group of poets gathered in the small village of Dymock in rural Gloucestershire, forming an interacting colony of talent. Included in their number were Lascelles Abercrombie, Wilfrid Gibson, Robert Frost, Rupert Brooke, John Drinkwater, Edward Thomas and Eleanor Farjeon. Among their visitors were W.H. Davies, Ivor Gurney and Edward Marsh, the influential literary promoter. Their move to Dymock was a conscious decision to work in and respond to the English countryside, to seek a literary idyll. The results were far-reaching. At the encouragement of Frost in particular, Edward Thomas turned from literary journalism, to become one of the greatest English poets of the century.

As often occurs with a LDR event, it was held on a Saturday morning and offered three route lengths, all held on Poets' Path I, Poets' Path II, and The Daffodil Way – distances ranging from 9 miles, 16 miles and a full marathon. The event is self-sufficient and with self-navigation, no marshalls are supplied en-route or indeed markers. A map is supplied with course details and instructions. Just my sorta thing, so I was looking forward to it.

The weather on the morning was cold and wet unfortunately. However, many were in good heart as we assembled at Dymock Church, where we listened to 'running poetry' by resident bard and fellow runner Kathy Tytler, before the start of the events at 9am.

The routes divided at various points and while we all went out the back of the church to a huge ploughed field after the second stile, runners/walkers moved off in various directions. I soon found myself on my own, with only my soggy map for company (help).

This was rural running at its best, very picturesque and to add value included a few hills. I discovered a schoolboy MX track (Bromsberrow) on my adventures and skirted Redmarley woods, before emerging opposite the church in the village itself. My next set of instructions were a bit vague and I was pondering my next move. Do I wait for some other runners to compare notes, or just push on with 16 mile option? The steady rain was slowly disintegrating my map and instructions, and with droplets of rain running off my nose I decided take the easy option and settle for the 9 miler.

Normally the end game is held at the cricket club, but with all the wet weather it was out of bounds as the finish and check-in point. Each course loop started and finished at race HQ. So as a temporary measure, the clocking-in point was a local primary school, which itself was a challenge to find! Tucked on the outskirts of the village over a railway line and all up hill. I was tempted just to jump in the car and drive home, but that risked a search party.

```
Time: 1.23
```

Running Log

Event: **Salisbury 10**

Distance: **10 miles**

Date: **13th March**

This early morning start was shrouded in thick fog, only becoming patchy when descending off the Marlborough Downs. Fortunately it had cleared to a wispy mist by the time I had found the race HQ.

The race started from the Five Rivers Leisure Centre, and immediately headed through the surrounding residential streets before hooking around to our left and heading out past Victoria Park. The field started to string out by the two mile mark, just after passing Hudson Field, with Old Sarum towering above us. We then escaped the city and headed out into the countryside and rural lanes. Passing through Salterton and making the 'turn' across a little bridge over the Avon at Upper Woodford.

Around eight miles, the route then dovetailed into the 'out route', giving a sense of just where I was and when to time my finishing effort. The route changed however, and threw me as we tucked into a footpath which ran alongside the nature Reserve and allotments. The swell of spectators welcomed the runners home, and I redoubled my efforts as the course tucked tightly for the run to the tape on a school athletic track.

Time: 1.36

Running Log

Event: **Reading Half Marathon**

Distance: **13.5 miles**

Date: **3rd April**

It was some 24 years later that I considered running the Reading Half Marathon again. My eldest son Jared, had got into distance running and between us thought that running the half marathon on my 56th birthday would be a wheeze. So out of race retirement again. Training had gone reasonably well and I'd managed a couple of 10-mile training runs. We all travelled up on the Saturday with us all, Naomi (Jared's wife) and Julie (my wife) checking in to a smashing B&B on the edge of the town. A restaurant in the centre of Reading was decided on for pre-race pasta loading (well, it is my Birthday). We had securely parked the car in a multi-story car park just off the town centre, a short walk from the Italian restaurant.

Our very enjoyable pig-out came to a sobering halt when we rounded the corner to find our multi-story had been locked up! Panic! How can get home (back to B&B)? Walking wasn't an option, not in these heels, neither was a taxi as we had to get to the start in the morning! Somehow my daughter In law had the presence of mind to have noticed and remembered an emergency phone number on a sign at the entrance. A call to this got through to a human who mercifully gave us the all-important code number which operated the steel shutter curtain. What a relief!

I can recommend the Reading Half Marathon, certainly its pre-race information and organisation, and certainly the race in general. An efficient car parking system has been introduced, which dependant on how much you paid, got you nearer to the finish line. We settled on a less expensive ticket which meant parking in the University Grounds with a park and ride function. April can be a chilly month, and we felt it as we walked the last quarter mile or so into Green Park. This a business park area,

Another half in the bag - something to smile about!

quite deserted, which made an ideal muster point and start line. However, the start on this occasion was possibly the worst I'd encountered. The

'pen system' on this morning simply didn't seem to work. The 2hr + group which I lined up in took some 21 mins to cross the start line after the hooter had sounded.

Leaving the business area and Green Park, the route heads out to the University campus, looping around its environs. Here is a good vantage point and has plenty of support. It also has a drinks station and a St Johns Ambulance post which unfortunately I had to stop at. I had picked up a blood blister on the ball of my foot which needed a lancing, followed by a good dollop of Vaseline, before popping my sock back on. Surprisingly the onward journey didn't feel too bad. The route edged into the town centre where great support helped dull any tenderness. Still, progress had gone well with my split times reasonable: 5k split: 25.43, 10k spilt: 62.16.

I reached Prospect Park in reasonable shape and was enjoying my Birthday, that was until that awful long drag back to the Madejski Stadium along Rose Kiln Lane (A33). Crowd support was sparse along this stretch and the goal of Reading FC football ground wasn't getting any nearer.

Finally I had made the ground and tried to up the pace for a final burst. The finish was inside the stadium where a finishing straight had been laid next to the pitch. Here was where the crowd were, a tremendous noise and finish environment, it was great, if I could just muster up a sprint finish.

Time: 2.09
Position: 3055/6920

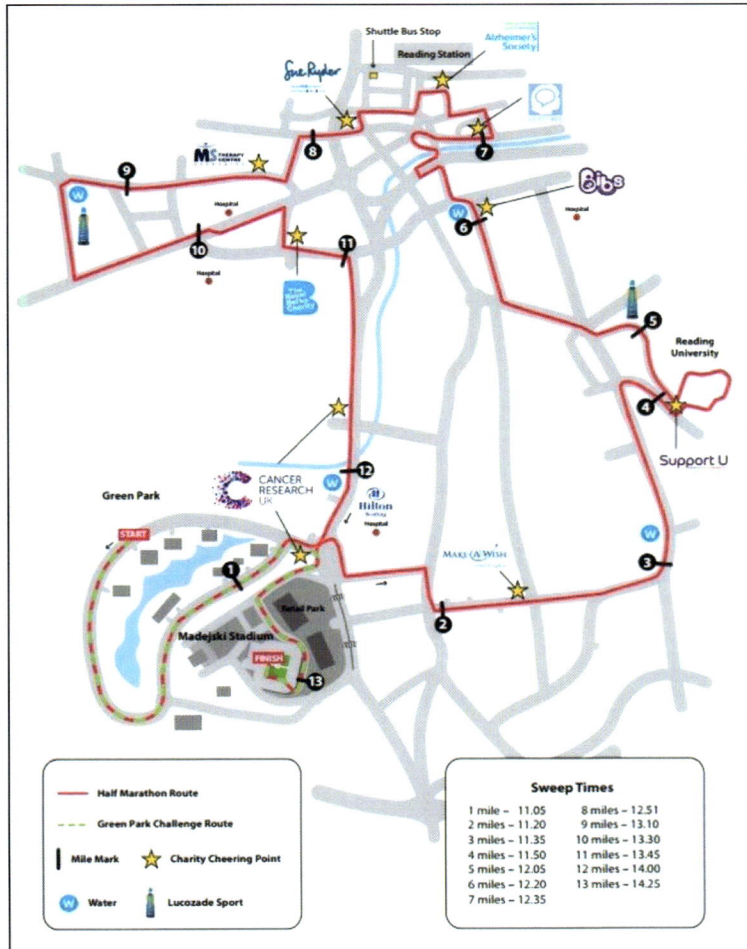

Reading Half marathon map

Running Log

Event: **Run the Rock**
Distance: **10K**
Date: **11th June**

Situated near Stokenchurch, the Run the Rock 10K course takes place on an undulating, mainly off-road course, with natural beauty throughout. In farm land the route includes tracks, fields and woods. The shade from the latter being particularly welcome on this day as it was sweltering temperatures. Many stiles interrupt your progress and the open chalk land reflects the heat. The only ones to be enjoying the thermals are the resident Red Kites.

Time: 1.06.26   Position: 102/149

Running Log

Event: **Oldbury Power Station 10**
Distance: **10 miles**
Date: **11th September**

Running in the shadow of a nuclear power station isn't something you do every day of the week, this one in particular is situated on the south bank of the River Severn. Gathering at the Power Station's clubhouse and buildings race HQ was busy. It's not a commonplace distance raced these days and like me I suspect a lot of last minute entries were in for a 'quick 10' before the local Bristol Half Marathon coming up.

It is renowned as fast and flat, and the early pace certainly suggested that. The course was made up of first a peculiar clockwise loop, the first taking the runners back towards the village of Oldbury before turning back towards the start. The second ran anti-clockwise, circling Shepperdine at six and seven miles. Definitely a good local race, well organised by the Thornbury Running Club.

Time: 1.33.42   Position: 174/232

Running is the curse of the drinking man.

HASH
HOUSE
HARRIERS

Running Log

Event: **Great Bristol Half Marathon**
Distance: **13.5 miles**
Date: **25th September**

Considering I had ran practically every half marathon on offer locally, for an inexplicable reason I had missed this West Country version. It saw life relatively late on, making its birth in 1989 with, just over the bridge, Welsh wizard Steve Brace winning. Local lad Nick Rose took the honours on its third running in 1991. These days, it shapes up under the Great Run banner with many thousands flocking to the Docks. The start and finish area was directly below my step daughter's top floor flat in Anchor Road. In years past a nuisance for her; closed roads and general inconvenience, this year a result! For me at least, as Julie (mum) and I could bunk down on Becky's floor with literally a hop & skip to the assembly area.

A nice table was reserved Saturday night for pasta loading in the city which also coincided with a Birthday treat for my wife, a perfect precursor to a good run, or so I hoped!

A chill in the air, but nevertheless a sunny autumn morning, as the Great Run Entrants huddled in the starting bays. The race snaked out of the Hotwells area and made its way down the Portway ducking under the wonder the of Brunel's suspension bridge. Things were going along quite nicely when suddenly, as I reached the turn (a cone to run round to send the runners back up the carriageway), I felt a pain in my calf.

I couldn't believe it. Apart from being injured I was at the furthest part of the course away from rescue or a pub to find solace.

I walked for a bit and stretched, still trying to decide what to do. I was being tracked, the new technology of a finishing chip also allowed Julie and Becky to check on my progress which had stopped. I had to get back into the city. Could I get going? Was I able to hobble to at least find my spouse?

Slowly, I managed to get going again with quite an exaggerated gait, it was a bit sore. I got back up to the swing bridge where the crowds were thick, and this helped spur me on, so I kept going. The long drag back up to Bedminster was tortuous, but here I saw Julie and Becky, completely unaware of my misfortune, so on I went. It was a great city run, lots of historical interest and large crowds as I made it over Redcliffe Hill and past the St Mary Church. I briefly saw Julie and Becky again - being able to track me meant they could short cut to wave me on at another vantage point. Now I was determined to finish. Over Bristol Bridge and onto Colston Avenue (this was before his nibs' Edward Colston statue was pulled down and chucked in the drink).

Just Anchor Road to go and a crescendo of noise as you drop down behind the watershed into the finishing straight. I was pretty beat up by the finish and I did some proper damage to my calf. Maybe I'll go back another year and run it on two legs!

```
Time: 2.11.05   Position: 4904
```

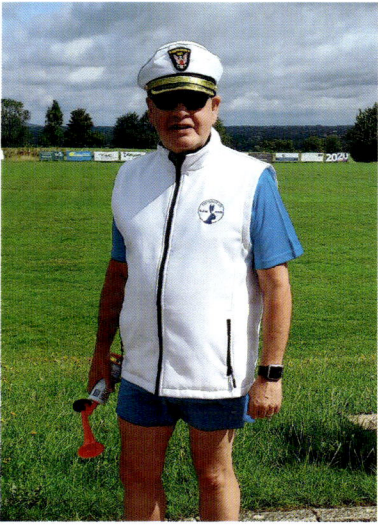

Running Log

Event: **Cobra Classic**
Distance: **10K**
Date: **11th June**

Organised by the Cobra Running and Triathlon club, this event had been running for several years under various guises. The race distance was also longer but with dwindling numbers the new look event reverted to the popular distance of 10K and took on a local Charitable Event, all monies raised going to Mary Stevens Hospice.

An added interest was a 5K prior to the main race which, after an arm twist, Jules (wife) took part in. A one-lap affair with the start from the excellent Old Halesonians RFC on the outskirts of Hagley. I was unsure of the name Cobra, but by the end of the race I can understand how it emerged, or maybe it was just a coincidence. But there was a sting in the tail. After a hurtle all down hill and a PB for the 5K the return was a hard climb back to the finishing line adjacent to the clubhouse.

```
Time: 59.58
(5K: 27.39)
Position: 85/124
```

Running Log

Event: **The Maverick inov-8 Original Sudeley Castle, Winchcombe**
Date: **17th June**

This seemed too good a chance to pass up - a traipse around the folds of the Cotswolds - my own back yard. Not a race, but a meander and to top it off, a race finish memento of a bottle of beer. This really was a throwback to the mid 80's, of the Beer Races where finishers would receive a can of Whitbread or Courage Light Ale.

Staged in Winchcombe with the magnificent backdrop of Sudeley Castle for the start and finish area. The event offered three lengths of cross country endurance running. A mass start took the field down across the stone bridge and out past the gate house. Avoiding the town, the runners turned left and immediately had a view of the size of hills which lay ahead.

A hot, dry, and dusty June made the ascent of Cleeve Common particularly tough. I noticed more experienced runners of this ilk of trailing had water bottles and camel packs hanging from every available part of their anatomy. The Maverick adventure trails, generally offer three lengths of trail around Long: 28km, Middle: 17 km and Short: 8 km, give a kilometre or two. Already thirsty - remember I was only in it for the beer - the first split came up, should I quit early? I wrestled with my conscience, had I deserved a beer yet? Too early to go back, I decided. There was an almighty climb next to a road which took the walkers (as most were now) up towards an ancient water wheel and across several farm land.

Eventually, after an arch high above, Winchcombe affording some splendid views. The route dropped back down beside Parks Farm and out onto Sudeley Hill. Crossing the road rather than drop back down the hill to the Castle, a footpath took the runners immediately back up another hill climb. The grassy meadows took me past fields of bleating sheep, and the ancient well of St Kenelms.

The route now levelled out and the final split appeared and yep here I chickened out. I took one look at the continued rise and waved the checkpoint marshal a good day and headed downhill. There was still some running left to do down through the meadows, the Castle in clear view as you follow a couple of footpaths which takes you back in a circuitous route, but at last the finish comes into view.

Across the finish line
If you're enjoying the escapades and have got this far you'll recognise my philosophy of how I enjoy my running. Many years ago now I took myself off the main roads (as much as I could), and made for the unbeaten track and sought many varying challenges, many you've already read about.

So here was an event I was perfectly in tune with, the good people at Maverick, chime well with my own sentiments "Our main objective is to get people off the roads and enjoying being outside in the countryside". The Maverick guys continue, "We're not elitist though which is why we've made them accessible to runners of all levels. With multiple route lengths to choose from in every location, you decide on the challenge", where a medal is soon dispensed followed next by a bottle of beer and - the best bit - the medal acts as a bottle opener – Genius.

Running Log

Event: **Hooky Six**
Distance: **Hook Norton Playing Fields**
Date: **6th August**

Hook Norton Harriers put on a very popular summer evening race around the picturesque village, including a tantalising glimpse of the Brewery on the two lap course. Starting from the Hook Norton Social Club, a virtually traffic-free course, described as undulating, I'd say hilly. In fact it was unexpected for many as droves dropped out after the first lap. To cap it all my wife beat me on the sprint for the line!

Julie ROBINSON Time: 01:09:14
Position 336
Graham ROBINSON Time: 01:09:16
Position 337

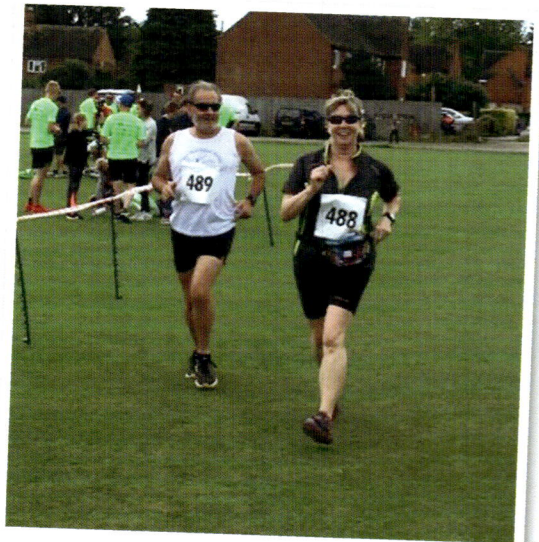

Jules out-sprinting me!

Running Log

Event: **Woodchester 8**
Distance: **8.4 miles**
Date: **3rd September**

Running Log

Event: **Cotswold Classic**
Distance: **10 miles**
Date: **17 September 2017**

A very tough multi-terrain event, set in the National Trust Area of Woodchester Park, organised by local Stroud & district AC. The start is a gallop downhill along a narrow stone-strewn track, which after it levels out, passes the incomplete Mansion House, before the fun begins.

The mansion was abandoned by its builders in the middle of construction, leaving behind a building that appears complete from the outside, but with plaster, floors, and whole rooms missing inside. It has remained in this state since the mid-1870s.

Steep climbs abound as the course winds through the canopy of trees. Stunning views of the lake and Boathouse do temper the agony going on in your legs. It's an out and back course, so you have the uphill finish to look forward to. Many club athletes participate, not an event for the faint-hearted.

Time: 1.28.54   Position: 85/89

Another event which involved a brewery, this time the Wychwood Brewery, and over the classic road race distance of 10 miles. Established for well over 30 years by the Witney Road Runners, it starts and finishes at the Kings School. Well organised and set on good safe roads, it incorporates the infamous 'Hillzakiller' which is a killer climb around 7–8 miles.

Time: 1.34.57
Position: 267/328

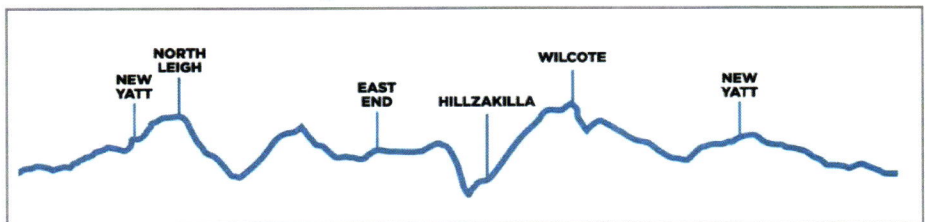

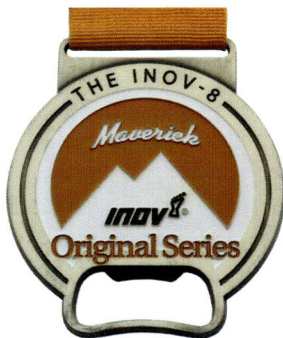

Worcestershire Midweek Series

Across the summer months, a few of the Midlands-based running clubs combine to put on a series of evening races. The races are organised over a variety of distance and terrains, around the 10K mark. All very enjoyable, and well supported with a good showing of spectators around each course. I entered all four, but only managed to compete in two of them, missing out on Hagley and Droitwich.

Running Log

Event: **Arrow Valley Redditch**
Distance: **12K**
Date: **13th June**

This is the largest open space in Redditch, acting as its' main lungs, with a lake and endless walks and park areas. It was the second race and well supported with plenty of space for runners. I did take a trip to earth as I clipped a tree root, but not too much damage, running well to the finish.

Time: 1.08

Running Log

Event: **Nimmings Wood, Clent Hills**
Distance: **8K**
Date: **1st August**

I'd not visited the Clent Hills before, but was very impressed with the scenery. Driving up the steep steep hill to the car park I could see this was not going to be easy!!

The race, which started under cover of the woods, soon struck out onto a plateau of winding trails which looked out across the vista. The course dropping violently and I was rueing the return as it was a two lap course of 4K. After it bottomed out, yes of course, we had to climb back toward the start/finish area. One section was vertical, and all but the leaders walked this section.

Time: 55.37 (very hard x2 laps)

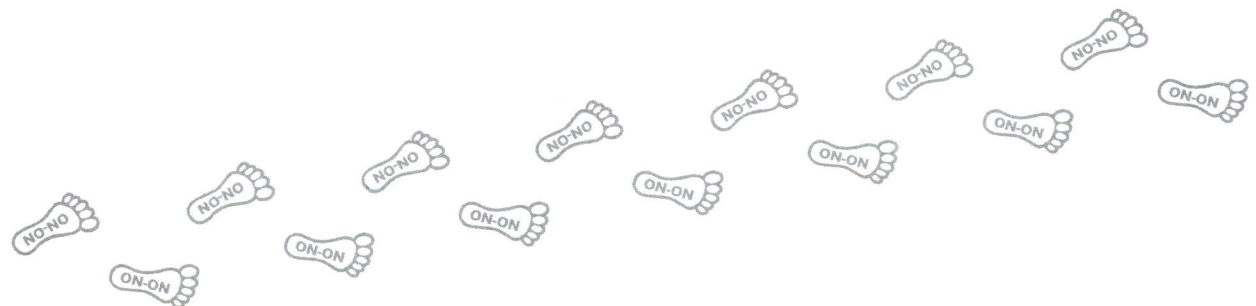

Pulmonary Embolism

It was the turn of the year when I got what I thought were heavy flu symptoms. In retrospect, although it was well before the charted curve of the Covid pandemic, all my symptoms were consistent with Covid 19. This 'bug' happened on January the 6th to be precise, and although it knocked any weekly runs, I did try to maintain a routine and stick at it.

However, one morning a week later on the Tuesday 15th after getting out of bed, my right calf suddenly went into a spasm, like a cramp. The morning trip to the bathroom was very uncomfortable. I put it down to a previous days run, and hope I hadn't pulled a muscle… now, hold that thought.

The weeks went by and no real improvement in my general fitness and my limbs were suffering, especially my hamstrings, particularly the left one. Maintaining three runs per week was proving difficult, as apart from my limbs I was also suffering from shortness of breath. It was now six weeks later when I decided to visit a GP. The outcome of this appointment resulted in me being prescribed steroids. The month now is March (4th) where I begin taking the prescribed drug, after two weeks I developed a consistent nose drip. I was still suffering with breathlessness and decided to come off the steroids, after a few days of withdrawal symptoms, aching and tiredness, I felt better. The weeks continued to go by and no breakthrough. Tight chest, breathless and the continuing nose drip and dry mouth, its now the back end of April. At this point after another GP visit it's thought that I may have developed asthma, so had to produce a peak flow test over the course of a few weeks. I was also given an inhaler (puffer).

I'm still trying to keep three runs a week up, but my weekly swim is becoming a problem as I can't breathe and swim a length without gasping and nearly drowning. However, suddenly during the middle of May I show some signs of improvement. Hashing with Bristol Greyhounds on the Monday in Thornbury (13th) did a steady four mile, plus two other runs and a NEW Cotswold hash on the Sunday (19th), another four miles. The following week was another improved week, an anomaly with four runs, including a 9 mile hash trail with Bicester at the weekend.

However, the following two weeks were dreadful, my running diary read: weds/fri two awful runs feel as if I'm right back to square one, and one interesting comment my arms ached! The hash run on 2nd June with NEW Cotswold from the Crown, Kemerton, read: poor start breathlessness / walk. Little better towards end.

Without realising it I was slowly grinding to a halt as my breathlessness continued to get worst. We were due to lay a hash trail two weeks later, and so on the 9th Julie and I walked and jogged our proposed run from Stanton. On several of the hills, however slight, Julie had to wait while I recovered as I was totally out of breath. On Wednesday 12th June I collapsed.

Julie and I had considered running that week with the Gloucestershire Gourmets hash group, and come the day in question I decided to 'check my fitness' I planned to pop to the post box during my lunch break to post some letters. The local shops of Mitton through a footpath are around 800 yards away – I didn't make it. I started to jog then walk and finally I collapsed in the alley, only coming to when a bystander is standing over me asking if I'm alright.

I took a severe bang on the head in my fall, which by medical consensus is possibly the reason that the heart was shocked into life. Julie had by now had managed to get to Tewkesbury and ride with me in the ambulance to Cheltenham General Hospital. If things weren't bad enough, a schizophrenic patient goes berserk on the ACU ward, but luckily Julie and my Son Craig escaped and alerted the medical team and security, whilst finding me a quieter area and bed for the night.

In the morning I cause panic as I wander off to the loo (unaided) and the nurse discovers an empty bed. I was on strict bed rest apparently. On the Thursday afternoon I was sent down for an MRI where even the guy in the white lab coat operating this wonderful all-seeing piece of technology could see the problem. Before I'd even got back into my wheelchair my new lab technician pal was of no doubt after he had viewed the scan. So that was the issue: mass collection of blood clots lining my lungs. It was so severe that my consultant, Adam Usher, informed me that I had so much blood in my lungs, only 30% capacity was left. This meant that a stay and a slow start to recuperation began on the Avening Ward which treats patients with respiratory conditions.

It was a chastening number of days, but made all the more bearable as I looked forward to Julie's regular visits, which were up-lifting and if she was worried, she never showed it. She was there as soon as visiting time was allowed, and didn't leave my side until she was told to go by the hospital staff. We both looked at making the most of life and beginning that long recovery together.

Many of the men on the ward were suffering the effects of years of smoking (if people saw what a habit of cigarettes could result in, no one would take up the deadly weed, it is pretty grim close up). I felt like a spring chicken in comparison to many of the guys, many permanently attached to air tanks.

I felt strong enough to go home in a couple of days, but Usher was having none of it and so I had a weekend stay at NHS' expense. One thing I couldn't complain about was the food. It was delicious; three square meals a day, the puds were always gorgeous.

I was eager to get out of Avening Ward and restlessly sat around awaiting my discharge on the Tuesday morning (18th June), the nurse informed me that I should be able to go home after the consultant had spoken to me. Sure enough, the consultant dropped by on his rounds. As he pulled the curtains around the bed my excitement was soon curtailed by his tone and cautionary message. What I hadn't expected was his assessment regarding my PE and its' effect on my heart, and the statement that it appeared only my fitness enabled my respiratory system and strong heart to survive – a 'normal member of the public' would have died. Pretty sobering stuff, but…

After my discharge it was home for more rest, something which I'm not renowned for, but as I soon discovered, progress back to some sort of reasonable fitness was going to take a while. The realisation that perhaps running may be a thing of the past, was a terrible dawning and while thankful that I survived, selfishly I wanted to be back to 'Robo normal'. But a simple walk to the shops proved a herculean task, and when on a fitness walk, found myself on a longer loop than I anticipated, I only just make it back home, collapsing wearily on the sofa and sleeping solidly for 12 hours.

Slowly, over the next few months things got better, and while my runs are at a more 'comfortable' pace, I'm really enjoying my running, particularly my hash trails with the N.E.W. Cotswold HHH.

The Covid Years Supplement
2020 - 2021

PANDEMIC: NO RUNNING. NO HASHING.

If surviving the Pulmonary Embolism on a personal level was a physical challenge, just to get back to feeling human again, the mental challenge of being cooped up indoors was on another level. If you recall we were allowed to leave our homes for just 20 minutes per day. Which, dear readers, is the reason you are halfway through reading the life and tales of a misspent jogger. And I'm sure a lot of people took up the mighty sword and tried their hand at this literary lark.

Of course the other challenge was to try and keep the NEW hash jogging along, without jogging!

Pretty soon the Global Pandemic had descended where the world of face coverings was going to be the norm. Covid hit and with it war-time restrictions, queues at supermarkets, shortages of foods, civil liberties confiscated, confusion and chaos on a whole new scale. Slogans and inept government instructions from a Downing Street lectern were doled out, from 'Stay At Home Saves Lives' to ''Eat Out To Help Out'. But with God's will I'm still here to tell that odd tale and write a book, so every cloud and all that...

During the early years of my running and training I ran into trouble a lot and frustratingly was bounding along one minute, and limping and in agony the next. This meant I frequently missed weeks of training and prep before many a big race which I'd hoped to run well in. I'm not sure if Marathons are quite the vogue that they were, it seems many have faltered or entries bombed, giving organisers a headache over finance.

The obvious race to buck the trend continues to be the London Marathon. So, after several 'spoilt attempts' at training properly for the Marathon I switched to a low mileage – long run strategy in an attempt to stay injury free. It worked only moderately. Fast forward to another Physio Visit, I am now armed with some relatively new information and an insight as to why I was so injury prone.

Looking back at my entries 'sore hip after hilly run' and another entry 'outside pain of left knee goes after a couple of miles' and 'very sore next day.' I still run regularly and still enjoy the freedom it gives and while not 'competing' any more, I still get injured regularly – or did.

Whilst not cured, ALL those issues I had decades before were explained in a sentence. So, a pair or orthotics were measured up and touch wood, although on very little mileage, I stay relatively injury free.

In the midst of writing this book, I realised that while I had got back to running (jogging) again. My attempt in keeping fit and in reasonable wobble shape, just to turn out for the hash was quite an effort. Satisfied that I was making progress from a SCB (short cutting bastard) to back marker and onto to MOOTH (middle order of the Hash) was contentment at first.

Reading back through my scribblings and reminisces I soon realised that I hadn't signed up for an actual race since 2018. Leaving aside the 3-year hiatus, following hard on its heels, the Covid pandemic. I wondered - should or even would I be able to contemplate a race again?

This did bother me and played on my mind a tad, I just wanted to get back to pre-PE, but it slowly dawned on me that might be that! With racing certainly out of the question.

We all know that running offers you that state of mind and often a pleasant distraction from the stresses of of life, and most of my escapades have given me the rush of a runner's high. I hadn't truly realised this until I reached this point. From the toughest of training runs and races. From the disappointment of missing a race due to a niggle injury. Somehow it's all worth it when the endorphin pings off your chest when you finish your run, or cross the finish line, and in my case the reward of a decent pint.

I realised a few years back that chasing PB's were for young buck athletes males and females. Just challenge yourself was my mantra, and complete at your level, finish the course first! There are plenty of sixty-somethings sat on couches with Netflix for company I reasoned with myself.

So in short, following my PE, any self confidence in my running prowess had long fled. The year had ticked by, and whilst I tried to add routine to any training I might do, break down soon followed. It was frustrating and demoralising, I didn't think I was 'overtraining' on such low weekly mileage, It just felt a hamster on a wheel syndrome.

As mentioned previously, keeping a training diary does enable you to pick up or identify any problems, which in your running keeps putting you on the sidelines. All my problems were lower leg issues, calf strain (mild), and night time cramps. I knew from experience that I wasn't running too hard or running in knackered trainers.

Then I realised that some medication that I was taking for cholesterol levels had an impact on muscle. Whist okay for the average Joe for a runner this was clearly proving a problem or so I thought. I contacted my consultant and she agreed immediately to stop taking the tablets which - touch wood - seems to have had an effect, as the muscle groups don't give up on me so readily and the night cramps diminished.

So I still had/have ambitions, although on a smaller scale, I wanted to try and complete (note subtle difference), not compete at another race.

Could I get that first race under my belt? Following my Pulmonary Embolism and the continued struggle to get fit, gain some running time, I was determined to do another race at least.

So, let me introduce you to The Mandy Whittington 9K. Mandy I discovered, was the founder of Newent Runners, who, after what was thought a routine varicose vein procedure, hit an unexpected complication with the saphenous vein, which inflamed and caused her death.

Running Log

Event: **Mandy Whittington**
Distance: **9K**
Date: **20th November**

This event is credit to Newent Runners for keeping her memory alive as well as providing a well-organised and challenging 10K (okay, 9.5 to be precise).

I arrived in Newent on a very crisp morning, but the frost was accompanied by clear blue skies. The advice to use the large car parks in town, and then take the short walk down to the Newent Community School to register, proved a good warm up. Starting on the school field we circumnavigated it before filing out onto the quiet country roads. A massive hill soon sorted the early pacesetters as many of us chugged slowly over the brow and past the old International Birds of Prey Centre on the outskirts of Cliffords Mesne. Some wonderful views could be enjoyed here before another short but stiff climb as we looped back towards Newent.

The course takes you around the outskirts of the forest town which does pick up some much-needed support. Somewhere along this stretch we enter Foley Road (previously the largest cul-de-sac in Europe), through the town centre, where many buildings date back to the 13th century, on past the half-timbered Market House (built in 1668), finally returning to the finish line at the School.

Time: 1.02.67 Position: 219/267

Running Log

Event:	**Kymin Fell Race, Monmouth**
Distance:	**4.42 Miles**
Date:	**Saturday 14 January 2pm**

To start the new year I wanted to 'get back to it' and after a few weeks of uninterrupted running decided to try my hand a local(ish) fell race.

Described as an ideal event for your first ever fell race. Fully marked with no chance of getting lost... IF you follow the arrows. I was used to following arrows, so lets give it a go! The Kymin is a high hill overlooking the town of Monmouth, which formed the focal point of this exhausting race. Perched on top of said hill is a round house which is the turning point on this up and down challenge. Being January, a recent snowfall had left pockets and drifts of snow in the woods high above our starting point. Also, a thick mist had just descended to make it more atmospheric and raw with cold.

Jules was arch supporter again on this one and had waved me off. In came the finishers showing various signs of falling en route, many muttering 'never again', or words to that effect. It was also sub-zero temperatures, so she had to keep marching up and down to stop freezing on the spot! The promise of a pub lunch in front of a roaring fire, thawed the pair of us out.

This was tough, I'd bitten off more than I could chew sprung to mind as I walked and trudged up the steep 1-in-1 ascent. Eventually the climbing stopped and a level section was enjoyed as I got my breath back, and was actually closing in on the group of runners ahead of me. Then as the route started to steeply descend I over-cooked it and went flying, landing heavily on my knee. It was tip toe from there onwards, but at least it was downhill if I could just stay on my feet! Organised by: Chepstow Harriers.

Time: 1.06.36   Position: 112/115

On the way down through the woods

Running Log

Event:	**Muddy Woody**
Distance:	**6 Miles**
Date:	**11th February 2024**

Wye Valley Brewery
MUDDY WOODY 6
288

Not really sure what inspired me to partake in this event, other than it came onto my radar, and what surprised me was that it had been running for 26 years. I wasn't sure how I'd missed it. Set in deepest Herefordshire, Haugh Woods to be accurate, and organised by the Wye Valley Harriers, I was tempted. So before you knew it race day was upon us and we set off.

With the wettest record rainfall for the UK over the last eighteen months, it was going to be damp underfoot, but no one could have envisaged the course conditions we encountered. The omens were there as Jules and I approached the start area and encountered a flood across the road. We allowed a van go through first to gauge the depth, and went for it.

The weather was actually quite chilly, but sunny. A short walk from the registration point at the start point, a warm up 'act' was in full flow: an aerobics work out to music (which is increasingly popular) - I just stretched.

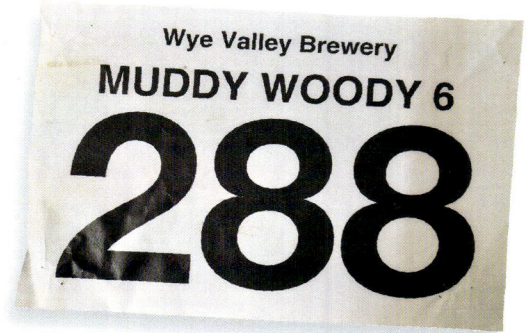

The organisers billed it as the iconic and original winter woodland race, somewhere in the small print it also stated this race is 'not for the faint-hearted'. It wasn't long before I could see what they meant. From an undulating start on a forest road of shingle, the route veered left up literally a wall of mud. Staying on one's feet was pretty difficult as the slop continued and got deeper and deeper.

The general euphoric vibe from the runners at the start soon dispersed, and only the Marshals remained cheerful as they cheered and clapped our efforts. The wooded glades were spectacular and some of the views from the tops of climbs were appreciated, although through gritted teeth.

Another fine mess – I've signed up for !!